# Chambers
# Card Games
# for Families
## The ultimate family pastime

## Peter Arnold

CHAMBERS
An imprint of Chambers Harrap Publishers Ltd
338 Euston Road, London, NW1 3BH

*Chambers Harrap Publishers Ltd is an Hachette UK company*

© Chambers Harrap Publishers Ltd 2011

Chambers® is a registered trademark of Chambers Harrap Publishers Ltd

This second edition published by Chambers Harrap Publishers Ltd 2011
First published in 2009, reprinted 2010

Database right Chambers Harrap Publishers Ltd (makers)

A CIP catalogue record for this book is available from the British Library.

10 9 8 7 6 5 4 3 2 1

ISBN 978 0550 10184 6

www.chambers.co.uk

Designed by Chambers Harrap Publishers
Printed and bound in Spain

# Contributors

### Author
Peter Arnold

### Chambers Editor
Anne Robertson

### Editorial Assistance
Lucy Hollingworth

### Prepress
Andrew Butterworth

### Illustrations
Andrew Butterworth
Andrew Laycock

### Publishing Manager
Hazel Norris

## About the author

Peter Arnold is an author and editor, most of whose 50 or so books concern sports and games. He has written histories and encyclopedias of boxing, cricket, football and the Olympic Games, and wrote the official FIFA guide to the 1994 Football World Cup in the USA. He has also worked as editor and main contributor of part-works on boxing and football, and has ghost-written instruction books for a West Indian Test fast bowler and a Canadian world snooker champion.

Peter devised some of the mental games for the television series *The Crystal Maze*. Several of his books are on table games, including some on individual card games, and he has written three books on gambling, one of which was described as 'the best history of gambling'. Many of his books have been published in the USA and in foreign-language editions.

# Contents

# Introduction by Peter Arnold

Why has the familiar pack of playing cards been so successful? How has the collection of 52 apparently simple designs of courtiers and symbols managed to bring so much pleasure to so many for over 600 years? Why do cards remain such a potent force for enjoyment even while competing against the shiny, sophisticated and expensive tools of modern entertainment: iPods, elaborate computer games, blockbuster films, television spectaculars and the like?

One answer is that few pastimes (and none of those just listed) offer such opportunities for interacting with companions in agreeable social circumstances as does a game of cards. For 'companions' one could substitute 'family'.

I suggest that nobody who played cards as a child with their parents, brothers or sisters ever forgets the games they played and the pleasure it brought them. They might not, on the other hand, have considered the benefits they might have gained as a result.

Playing cards on an equal footing with adults gives children self-esteem, promotes confidence in their ability and intelligence, gives them a sense of social behaviour, provides practice in winning and losing and how to accept both, and in a young child can even help with learning numbers and simple arithmetic. And, of course, in more advanced games it fosters mental agility in considering tactics and probabilities.

For these reasons *Chambers Card Games for Families* has been produced. Its contents cover, in the main, card games which the whole family, young and old, can play together, plus several which the younger members could play on their own. This is not to say that all the games are simple ones free from the need for skill. Indeed some are almost certain to be won by the best player.

The description of each game is headed by a panel which offers vital information to players choosing a game to play, such as the number of players suitable for the game. The number of players is always the first limiting factor on the choice of game – if there are, say, five players, games designed specifically for three or four are ruled out. If games can be played by any number of players it is sometimes suggested which numbers are considered best.

It might be thought strange that a collection of games for families includes four patience games. The reason is that there are times when the whole family do not wish to play at once, and even if the number drops to one, there is an amusement here to satisfy.

In the information panel heading each game the lines which read 'Minimum age' and 'Skill factor' were the hardest to write. The minimum age is based on the complexity of the game and how much card-playing nous is required to play it. The minimum age range in this book stretches from six to twelve years old. It is based on subjective opinion, and of course there will be parents who point out that their young prodigy could play such-and-such a game at a much younger age than that specified. There will also be indignant parents affronted that their eight-year-old cannot grasp the nuances of a game said to be suitable for seven-year-olds. To both sets apologies are offered plus an acknowledgement that they know their child's abilities better than the writer.

The skill factor of a game is also difficult to assess, as it is only partially related to its complexity. The amount of skill required to play a game well can be measured by how regularly the best players will win. Pelmanism illustrates the difference between the age factor and the skill factor. It is a game of such simple rules that a six-year-old could play it. But it is a game where chance plays a minimal part, and the player with the best memory for where the cards lie will nearly always win. It is thus a very skilful game. The skill factor in these descriptions is therefore often a little vague, but combined with the minimum age recommendation it is hoped that it will provide a reasonable guide to adults as to whether a game is suitable for the age range of their family or not.

More about playing games with children appears on p163.

It is hoped that this book will promote the enjoyable playing of cards within the family and thus help prolong the popularity of playing cards perhaps for another 600 years.

Peter Arnold

# Card Games

# Accordion

Accordion is the simplest of all patience games, so simple that it probably wasn't invented consciously but just evolved, or – more accurately – just happened. It has acquired the name Accordion because it takes place in one line of cards that during the game tends to get longer and shorter, rather like the way an accordion does when it is being played.

| | |
|---:|:---|
| **Alternative names** | Idle Year, Methuselah |
| **Players** | One |
| **Minimum age** | Seven years old |
| **Skill factor** | Little judgement needed |
| **Special requirements** | A moderately large space |

## Aim
To end with all 52 cards in one face-up pile.

## Preparation
A single pack of cards is shuffled and held face down in the hand.

## Play
Cards are turned over one at a time and played to the table. The first is dealt to the top left of the available playing space. The second card is played to its right and the third to the right of that and so on, so that the 'tableau', if it can be so called, is a single line of cards, or piles of cards.

A card that is played to the right of a card that it matches in either suit or rank can be packed upon it. Similarly, if a card matches in suit or rank a card third to its left, it can be packed upon it (ie the card will have to jump over two other cards). Those are the only two moves allowed. A move must always be made when possible. Sometimes a card can be packed in either of these two places, when the player must decide which of the two is preferable. Sometimes one move allows another, and the turn of one card might provoke several moves and shorten the 'accordion' accordingly.

When a card is the top card of a pile, then it governs the whole pile, and if it can be moved to the left it takes the whole pile with it – the pile should never be split. When a gap in the line is created by moving a card or pile forward along the line, then the card or cards to the right move to the left to close the gap. If the line gets so long that there is no space for further cards then a second line is started below the first, but the two lines must be considered as one continuous line.

The game ends when all the cards from the hand are dealt to the table. The game is won if there is only one pile on the table. If more, it is lost.

Accordion is a difficult game to win, and can be very frustrating, as you can approach the end with perhaps only three or four piles on the table and then deal seven or eight cards in a line, none of which can be moved.

**Example game**

Suppose there is a line of five piles, as illustrated.

Tableau

Next card

The next card turned up is the ♣9. The ♣9 is played to ♣7, and that pile played to ♦9. Then ♣K is played to ♣9 and then to ♠K. The accordion is then reduced to two piles, headed by ♣K and ♦3. If the next card is ♦K or ♣3, then the piles would be reduced to one. Notice, however, that if in the position shown, the ♣9 had been played to the ♣K instead of the ♣7, the only other move possible would have been ♣9 to ♦9, and the accordion would be left with four piles instead of two.

# Bango

Bango was invented when the game of bingo became a craze in Great Britain in the 1960s, and is an attempt to use playing cards to bring some of the atmosphere of the bingo hall to the home. It is necessarily played for smaller stakes but is a fair game of pure luck with equal chances of winning or losing over a long period. It can be played with children for counters.

| | |
|---|---|
| **Alternative names** | None |
| **Players** | Three to ten, the more the better; for more than ten, see Variants |
| **Minimum age** | Seven years old |
| **Skill factor** | No skill needed |
| **Special requirements** | Cash, chips or counters for staking; a bowl or saucer to hold the pool of stakes |

## Aim
Each player aims to win by being the first to turn all his face-up cards face down.

## Cards
Two standard packs of 52 cards are required for up to ten players. It is convenient if the packs have different backs, as they should not be mixed.

## Preparation
Any player may pick up one pack of cards and shuffle. Another cuts and deals one card face up to each player to decide the first dealer – the player who receives the first Jack is the first dealer. There is no advantage or disadvantage to being the dealer.

Each player puts an agreed amount into the bowl to form a pool. The dealer and the player to his left each shuffle a pack of cards, and the player to the dealer's right cuts each pack.

## Play
The dealer takes one pack and deals the cards singly to each player, including himself, until each has five cards. The players arrange their cards face up in a row before them. The dealer then puts the first pack aside.

The dealer then takes the second pack of cards and deals the top card face up to the table, announcing its rank and suit. If any player, including the dealer, has among the cards in front of him the card from the first pack which matches the dealt card in both rank and suit he turns his card face down.

The dealer then deals the second card face up to the table, announcing it in the same manner, and a player whose cards include the identical card from the first pack turns it face down, and so on.

As soon as a player has turned over all five of his cards, he calls 'Bango'. The dealer then checks that all the turned-over cards have their match among the cards he dealt. The first player to turn over all five of his cards takes the pool.

### Variants

If there are more than ten players, then a third pack must be employed. Two packs with identical backs are required to deal out the players' hands, while the third pack, with a different back, is used for the dealer to indicate the winning cards.

It may be that a player's hand, when two packs are used to provide it, may include two identical cards, but this does not matter. If the matching card is turned up by the dealer, the player turns face down both of his identical cards.

It could happen, but rarely, that two players could call 'Bango' at the same time. In this case they share the pool.

# Beggar My Neighbour

Beggar My Neighbour is a very simple children's game – often the first game that children learn – and probably arises from an early gambling game. There is no skill involved and the outcome depends entirely on luck.

| | |
|---|---|
| **Alternative names** | Beat Your Neighbour Out of Doors, Strip Jack Naked |
| **Players** | Any reasonable number |
| **Minimum age** | Six years old |
| **Skill factor** | No skill needed |
| **Special requirements** | None |

### Aim
To capture all the cards in the pack.

### Cards
The standard pack of 52 cards is used.

### Preparation
A dealer is chosen by any method. The cards are shuffled and dealt clockwise face down, beginning with the player to the dealer's left, one at a time to all players including the dealer until all the cards are exhausted. It does not matter if some players have more cards than others.

### Play
The players take their cards into their hands, holding them in a face-down pile. Beginning with the player to the dealer's left, each player plays the top card of his hand face up to the table one on top of the other to form a central pile. There are 16 honour cards: the Ace, King, Queen and Jack of each suit. When an honour is played, the following player has to cover it with a specific number of other cards:

| | | | |
|---|---|---|---|
| Ace | four cards | Queen | two cards |
| King | three cards | Jack | one card |

If while doing this he deals an honour, then the following player has to cover the new honour at the same rate: four for an Ace and so on. If an honour is played and the required number of cards are played to it without another honour appearing then the player of the honour takes the whole of the pile from the table and adds them face down to the bottom of the stack of cards in his hand. The player nearest his left then begins a new round of play.

A player who has played all his cards to the table retires from the game. If he runs out of cards while fulfilling the obligations in playing to an honour, then the player of the honour takes the pile as usual.

Gradually the players are knocked out of the game one by one, until only one is left and is declared the winner.

**Beggar My Neighbour**

# Bismarck

How Bismarck got its name is a mystery, but it is a good game for three which deserves to be better known. Despite its German name it was said to be popular with British soldiers.

| | |
|---|---|
| **Alternative names** | Sergeant Major (see Variants) |
| **Players** | Three |
| **Minimum age** | Twelve years old |
| **Skill factor** | A skilful game |
| **Special requirements** | Pen and paper for scoring |

## Aim
To score points in a variety of trick-taking games, by winning (or in one deal, losing) tricks.

## Cards
The standard pack of 52 cards is used, the cards ranking from Ace (high) to 2 (low).

## Preparation
The shuffled pack is spread face down, and each player draws a card, the drawer of the highest becoming the first dealer. If there is a tie, the joint highest draw again.

## Play
The dealer shuffles and the player to his right cuts. The dealer deals 16 cards to each player, one at a time face down clockwise to his left. The last four cards he adds to his own hand. Before the first lead, the dealer must discard four cards from his hand face down so that each player has 16 cards. The 'eldest hand' (the player to the dealer's left) leads to the first trick and the winner of a trick leads to the next. The usual rules of trick-taking apply; see p155 for an explanation of tricks and trick-taking. Each player must follow suit to the card led if able, and if unable may play a trump (if there are trumps) or discard. The trick is won by the highest trump it contains or, if there aren't any, by the highest card in the suit led.

Each dealer deals for four rounds in succession, each of which is played in a different manner, as follows:

| | |
|---|---|
| *Deal 1* | This hand is played without trumps. The object is to score as many tricks as possible. |
| *Deal 2* | The dealer turns over the last of the four extra cards he deals |

himself, and this card denotes the trump suit for the deal. The object is as before.

*Deal 3*    The dealer, after examining his hand and discarding his four extra cards, chooses the trump suit for the game. The object is as before.

*Deal 4*    There are no trumps, and the object is to win as few tricks as possible.

**Scoring** There is clearly an advantage to the dealer in each of the deals, if only in his extra choice of cards, and the method of scoring reflects this.

In the first three deals, the dealer scores one point for every trick he makes above eight, while his opponents (who play individually) each score one point for every trick they make above four. In the fourth deal, the dealer scores four points minus the number of tricks he took, while his opponents each score six points minus the number of tricks they took.

Points are entered on a scoresheet after each deal, and the winner is the player with most points when each player has dealt for each of the four types of deal (ie a game consists of twelve deals).

**Example hand**

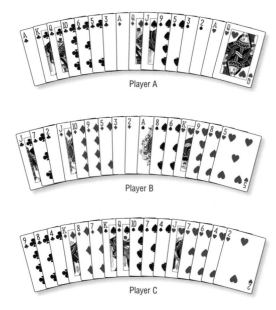

Player A

Player B

Player C

In the illustration, Player A was the dealer in deal 3. He announced clubs as trumps and discarded ♦6, 4 and ♥10, 3 from his 20 cards. Player B, who is the eldest hand, leads ♠A and play continues:

| | Player A | Player B | Player C |
|---|---|---|---|
| 1 | ♠2 | ♠A | ♠4 |
| 2 | ♠3 | ♠8 | ♠K |
| 3 | ♠5 | ♠6 | ♠Q |
| 4 | ♠J | ♣2 | ♠10 |
| 5 | ♦Q | ♦2 | ♦7 |
| 6 | ♣A | ♣7 | ♣4 |
| 7 | ♣K | ♣J | ♣8 |

It can be seen now that Player A will make all the remaining tricks except one, as only the ♥Q is not a master. He will lose ♥Q to Player B's ♥K. Player A will therefore win 11 tricks for three points. Player B will win three tricks and Player C two tricks, so neither will score any points.

## Variants

**Sergeant Major** (also called 8-5-3) is a variant of the above. The changes are as follows:

i) Each deal is played as deal 3 above, ie the dealer names the trump suit. The last four cards in the deal he places face down on the table instead of taking them into his hand. He names the trump suit before he discards four cards and takes up those from the table.

ii) The dealer's target is eight tricks, the eldest hand's target is five tricks and the other player's target is three tricks.

iii) As well as winning one point for each trick won above his target, a player loses one point for each trick below his target. It is best to give each player 20 points on the scoresheet to start, thus obviating the need for minus scores.

iv) On each deal, a person who takes more tricks than his target is regarded as 'up' for the following deal, while a player who takes fewer tricks than his target is regarded as 'down'.

v) On each deal, if any player was up on the previous deal, an exchange of cards takes place before the dealer has added to his hand the four additional cards dealt to the table. If there was one player who was up, he exchanges a card or cards with each player who was down, according to the number of cards that player was short of his target. For each card he is given, the down player must return to the up player his highest card in that suit (it is possible he may have to return the same card given him). If there are two down players, the up player exchanges cards first with his left-hand opponent. If there are two players up, each exchange cards with the down player, beginning with the player who has the higher target in the current deal. When the exchange of cards has taken place, the dealer names trumps, discards four cards from his hand, and picks up the four cards on the table.

1

vi) The game ends when one player (it is likeliest to be the dealer) takes twelve or more tricks in a deal, the winner being the player with the highest number of points after the last score is added. It is not as unlikely as it might seem for a dealer to make twelve tricks, as his target is eight anyway. If he is on a winning streak he will improve his hand by exchanging with the other players even before he discards his four worst cards to the table. The example hand at Bismarck above shows how feasible it is.

A variant of Sergeant Major is sometimes played with the targets for the three players being nine for the dealer, five for the eldest hand and two for the third player, with the alternative name of 9-5-2.

# Casino

Nobody knows how Casino acquired its name. The assumption is that it was simply named after a casino, where it might have been found as a gambling game. Whether this is true or not, many people also spell it Cassino, with a double 's', and it appeared as Cassino in its first description in English in 1797. Ever since there have been writers who wish to correct the 'printer's error', and others (the majority) who prefer Cassino, on the grounds that even if it were a misprint it is a fortuitous one, distinguishing the game from the building. Here Casino has been chosen as it was preferred by the late George F Hervey, an expert on card games.

Casino is believed to have originated in Italy, where it would be played with the 40-card Italian pack, ie one lacking the 8s, 9s and 10s. It is often thought of as a children's game, but it is a game of skill, where a player who can memorize the cards played has an advantage.

| | |
|---|---|
| **Alternative names** | None |
| **Players** | Two; three or four for Variants |
| **Minimum age** | Eight years old |
| **Skill factor** | Skill is needed to play well |
| **Special requirements** | Pen and paper for scoring |

## Aim
To score the most points; points are won by capturing the majority of cards from the layout, with particular attention to certain cards which carry bonuses.

## Cards
The standard pack of 52 cards is used. The numeral cards count their pip values. Aces count as one. Court cards have no numerical value and are used only to make pairs.

## Preparation
The players cut a spread pack, and the player who cuts the higher card (King high, Ace low) is the first dealer.

The dealer deals two cards face down to his opponent, two face up to the table layout, then two face down to himself. He repeats this so that both hands, and the table layout, contain four cards. The table layout is four cards in a line. The remaining cards are placed face down on the table.

## Play
Each player, beginning with the non-dealer, plays a card in turn until their hands are exhausted. The same dealer (who deals throughout) then takes the pack and

Casino

deals another four cards to each player, two at a time as before, but none to the layout (which is replenished during play, as will be seen below). The process is repeated each time the hands are exhausted until, after six deals, the pack itself is exhausted. Before the last deal the dealer must announce 'Last'.

During the play, players capture cards from the layout. These cards, together with the cards that capture them, the player keeps face down beside him until the end of the hand.

Occasionally during play, the layout is temporarily denuded of cards. This is called a 'sweep'. The player who captures the card or cards which causes the sweep, turns one of the cards face up when adding them to his captured pile. This enables him at the end of the hand to count his total of sweeps, each of which earns a point.

A player has four choices of play, as follows:

*Pairing*  A player may pair a card from his hand with a card or cards from the layout and thus capture them. For example, if the layout contains one or more 3s, and the player has a 3 in his hand, he may use his 3 to capture them. He shows his 3, picks up the 3s from the layout and places the cards before him face down. This is the only way in which court cards can be captured.

*Combining*  A player may capture two or more cards from the table with a card the pip total of which equals the sum of the pip totals of the cards. For example, an 8 can capture a 6 and a 2, or a 4, 3 and Ace. As with pairing, a player can capture more than one combination with the same card, and may capture cards by both pairing and combining at the same time; for example, an 8 could capture an 8 (pairing) plus two 4s (combining). Note, however, that a card in the layout cannot be counted twice, ie as part of two combinations. For example, if the layout contained 6,3,3,3, a player holding a 9 could use it to capture the three 3s, or the 6 and a 3, but cannot capture all the cards, as that would involve counting one of the threes twice.

*Building*  A player, instead of capturing, may play a card to the layout which will allow him to capture on a future turn. For example, if there is a 3 in the layout, and the player holds a 5 and an 8, he may play the 5 to the 3 on the layout, overlapping the cards and saying 'building 8s', intending to take the two cards on a future turn. He must hold the card which will allow him to capture – he cannot build 8s without holding an 8 in his hand. This is called a 'simple build'.

He is not obliged to capture the build on his next turn, and may prefer to make another capture first, particularly if his opponent makes a build which he himself can capture. A build is not the property only of the player making it.

A player can make a 'multiple build' by adding other cards to the layout. For example, in the instance above, where a player adds a

14

5 to a 3 in the layout to build 8s, he could also play a 7 to an Ace to the layout on his next turn, with the intention of capturing all four cards with his 8 on a future turn.

A player can also make a multiple build on a single card. Suppose there is a 6 in the layout, and the player holds two 6s. Instead of using one 6 to capture that in the layout, thus capturing two cards, he could play one of his 6s to the 6 in the layout and announce 'building 6s'. On his next turn he could then capture both 6s in the layout with his remaining 6, thus capturing three cards rather than two. In the same way, if he holds two 6s and the layout includes a 4 and a 2, he can combine the 4 and 2 and play one 6 to them announcing 'building 6s', enabling him to capture all three cards next turn with his remaining 6.

A build can also be increased. Suppose there is a 3 in the layout, and the player holds a 6 and a 9, he can play the 6 to the 3 and build 9s. If he also has an Ace and a 10, he can on his next turn add the Ace to the build and announce 'building 10s', using his 10 on his next turn to capture all three cards. As 10 is the highest card in the pack, it follows that a build cannot exceed ten.

As stated, a build is not the property of the player making it, and as well as capturing his opponent's build, a player may add to it. Suppose the opponent is building 7s, and a player holds a 9 and a 2. He can add the 2 to the build and announce 'building 9s'. Building on an opponent's build is a good move, since it not only provides three cards in the layout which can be captured, but leaves the opponent holding a card (in the example a 7) which he now cannot use.

It is not permitted, however, to increase a multiple build. For example, if a player building 6s has a 4 and a 2, and also a 5 and an Ace, in the layout, it is not permitted to add a card to one of the builds to increase it further. Note the difference between a multiple build and a simple build. If, for example, a player builds a 3 to another 3, and announces 'building 3s', in order to take both 3s with a third 3, that is a multiple build which therefore cannot be built on. However, had he announced 'building 6s', with the intention of taking both 3s with a 6, that is a simple build, and can be built on, for example by playing a 2 to it and announcing 'building 8s'.

Once a card is part of a build, it cannot be captured individually. For example, if a 2 in the layout has had a 3 added to it by a player building 5s, neither the 2 not the 3 can be captured by a player holding another 2 or 3.

It is worth emphasizing that to make a build, the player must hold in his hand a card to take it. If, for example, there is a 5 in the layout, and a player holds A, 2, 8, Q, he cannot add the Ace to the 5 and announce 'building 6s', and next turn add the 2 and announce 'building 8s', with the intention of taking all three cards with his 8, because he does not hold a 6 which would have permitted him to build 6s in the first place. A player who builds without holding the requisite card in his hand automatically loses the game.

*Trailing*   If a player on his turn cannot pair, combine or build, he must 'trail', which is to add a card from his hand face up to the layout. This is how the layout is replenished, and may become larger than the original four cards. A player may trail even if he is able to pair, combine or build, unless he has a build in the layout, when he is obliged to capture it before he can trail.

When a sweep occurs, and the layout is cleared of cards, the next player has no option but to trail.

**Scoring**   Points are scored as follows:

*Cards*   The player who captures the majority of the cards (ie 27 or more) scores three points.

*Spades*   The player who captures the majority of the spades (ie seven or more) scores one point.

*Big casino*   The player who captures the ♦10 scores two points.

*Little casino*   The player who captures the ♠2 scores one point.

*Aces*   A player scores one point for each Ace captured.

There are therefore eleven points at stake to be won in this manner, though the points for cards are not scored if each player captures 26 cards.

A further point is scored for each sweep recorded by each player, ie for each time a player clears the layout. As mentioned earlier, this is best recorded by turning a card in the captured pile face up – each face-up card represents a point.

If there are cards in the layout when all play has finished, then the player who made the last capture takes them. This does not count as a sweep, but the cards count in all the categories.

**Game**   Games can be played as one deal (ie until the pack is exhausted), in which case the player with the most points wins. Otherwise the game is to 21 points. In this case it is best to play every deal to the end, then count each player's points in the order set out above, from cards down to sweeps, and then add them to the previous total.

When players approach 21 the points should still be taken in this order, and hence someone might win with 21 having scored three points for cards first, even if the opponent would score the next five points and finish with a higher total overall.

**Example hand**
The layout and hands are dealt as shown below.

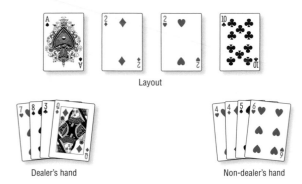

Layout

Dealer's hand                                    Non-dealer's hand

The non-dealer has a number of options on his first turn. He can capture the A, 2, 2, with his 5. Or he could add the two 2s together and play a 4 to them announcing 'building 4s', with the intention of taking all three cards with his other 4. He could play his 5 to the Ace and announce 'building 6s', and take them with his 6 next time, leaving the 2s and 4s to be taken later.

He decides on the first course, since he wants to make sure of the Ace for a point, and by doing this he captures four cards, including the Ace and two spades. Notice that had he left the Ace untouched, the dealer would have played his 7 to it, building 8s, and would have captured it himself.

The non-dealer therefore captures ♠A, ♦2, ♥2 with ♠5. The dealer trails his Queen. The non-dealer trails ♦4, intending to capture this 4 with his other 4 next turn. The dealer builds ♣3 onto ♦4, announcing 'building 7s', thus thwarting the non-dealer's plan; instead the non-dealer now trails ♥4. The dealer captures ♦4, ♣3 with ♥7. The non-dealer trails ♥6. The dealer trails ♠8.

So after the first hand, the non-dealer has captured four cards, including an Ace and two spades, and the dealer three. There are five cards in the layout. The dealer now picks up the non-used part of the pack and deals four cards to each two at a time, and play begins again.

**Variants**
Some players prefer not to count scores for sweep on the grounds that sweeps are gained more by luck than judgement, and the points for sweep unbalance the scores.

**Casino for three players** Casino is played by three players in exactly the same manner as for two, with each player playing for himself. There are only four hands each per deal, ie before the pack is exhausted. The 'eldest hand' (the player to the dealer's left) plays first and the dealer last. It is considered that the eldest hand and the dealer have an advantage over the other player, so it is fairer not to play to a set total of points, but to total the scores after each player has dealt once. If there is a tie on the count for cards or spades, no points are scored.

**Casino for four players** Casino can be played by four players in partnerships of two, with partners sitting opposite each other. While partners combine the points made in captures, the rules are exactly the same as in the basic game. For example, a player seeing his partner build 7s, say, cannot himself build a 7 for his partner to take, without himself holding a 7. There will be only three hands per deal. Players can agree on the length of a game. It could be of 21 points, or a number of deals: one per side, or one per player.

**Royal Casino** Royal Casino is often thought to be a better game than the parent game in that more skill and concentration are required. There are two differences. Court cards are given values and treated like the other cards: Jack counts as 11, Queen as 12 and King as 13. In addition Ace can count as 1 or 14 at the discretion of the player. Thus 6, 4, 3 might be captured with a King, or it might have an Ace added to it, building 14s, which could be captured by another Ace. Scoring is as for the parent game, and two to four people can play.

**Spade Casino** Spade Casino is played the same way as the basic game, but with a change to the scoring. Instead of the category spades, in which a player or side scores a point for the majority of spades, one point is awarded for each spade captured, with an extra point for the Jack. As the ♠A and ♠2 also earn an extra point for being an Ace and little casino respectively, this means that ♠A, J and 2 are worth two points each, the other spades one. The total points available, excluding sweeps, is thus 24 (as opposed to eleven in the parent game). If not played to an agreed number of deals, the game is played to 61 points, which makes a Cribbage board (see the illustration at Cribbage on p32) a convenient means of scoring.

**Draw Casino** Draw Casino introduces a different method of dealing which can be applied to any of the variants above. After the first deal of the hands and layout, the remaining cards are placed in the centre face down to form a 'stock'. Each time a player plays a card he draws the top card of the stock to replace it. By this means each player's hand remains at four cards, and no further deals are necessary. When the stock is exhausted, each player plays his last four cards in the usual way.

Casino

# Cheat

Cheat is a very simple children's game, not to be taken too seriously.

| | |
|---|---|
| **Alternative names** | I Doubt It |
| **Players** | Three to eight; five to eight is best |
| **Minimum age** | Seven years old |
| **Skill factor** | No skill needed |
| **Special requirements** | None |

## Aim
To get rid of all the cards in your hand.

## Cards
The standard pack of 52 cards is used.

## Preparation
From a pack scattered face down on the table, each player draws a card to determine the first dealer. The drawer of the highest card deals. Cards for this purpose rank from Ace (high) to 2 (low). If two or more players tie for highest card they draw again.

The dealer deals one card at a time face down to all players until the pack is exhausted. It does not matter if some players receive one card more than others.

## Play
The players take their cards into their hands. The player to the dealer's left then plays up to four cards, of any rank or suit, face down in a fan to the centre of the table. At the same time he announces how many cards are being played and that they are of the same rank, for example calling 'four 2s', 'one King' or 'two 9s'. The player can either announce correctly what he has played, or can choose to lie. Thus three cards played and announced as 'three Aces', for example, may indeed be three Aces; but they may instead comprise A, 2, 6, or 3, Q, K, or any other combination of cards from the player's hand.

The next player clockwise must then play up to four cards face down to the first card, and announces them as the next higher value. For example, if the first player had announced 'one 6', the next player must announce between one and four '7s'. The following player must then play a card or cards and announce a number of '8s', and so on. The sequence is endless, with Ace following King. These cards might be played as announced or they might not, as each player can lay whatever cards he likes. Indeed, he may not even hold a card of the denomination required, and is therefore forced to lie.

At any time a player who thinks that an opponent has lied in announcing the

**Cheat** (side tab)

value of the card or cards played may call out 'cheat'. The card or cards are then turned over for all to see. If the player did indeed cheat, and the card or cards are not what he announced, then the one who cheated must pick up all the cards on the table and add them to his hand. The player who successfully called him then leads a card or cards to start a new round, announcing the rank (either truly or falsely, as desired).

If the player called did not cheat and the card or cards are what was announced, then the player who wrongly called 'cheat' must pick up all the cards and add them to his hand, while the virtuous player who was falsely accused leads to a new round.

If more than one player calls 'cheat' and there is an argument as to who was first, the one sitting nearest to the left of the accused is regarded as first.

If a player has lied about the cards played, but no one calls 'cheat' and the next person plays his cards to the table, he has cheated successfully and cannot be called a 'cheat' retrospectively. He is the only one to know of his deception, and smugly continues to play in the usual way.

As soon as a player realizes that to call 'cheat' risks having to pick up all the cards, and that it is best to allow somebody else to shout 'cheat', then he is getting too old for the game. But young children get fun out of accusing others of cheating. Parents should appreciate that if a player laying down his last card is accused of 'cheating', as he always should be, it is extremely likely that he is cheating, and will have to pick up the cards. So the game continues ... and continues ...

**Variants**

Some people play that only one card can be put down at a time, making for an even lengthier game.

Alternatively, some people play that any number of cards can be put on the table at one go, but, as they must be announced as the same rank, four remains the maximum that can be announced. This necessitates some skill on the part of players placing cards on the table to ensure that a carefully arranged fan of 'four' cards isn't nudged as it is put down to reveal other cards hidden beneath. This kind of audacious cheating often causes great hilarity when discovered, but can lead to ever more outrageous attempts to cheat, leaving the game to descend into outright silliness.

# Chinese Ten

Chinese Ten is a game that basically requires the ability to spot pairs of numbers which add up to ten. A little skill is required in choosing which is the better when there are alternative choices of play.

| | |
|---|---|
| **Alternative names** | None |
| **Players** | Two to four |
| **Minimum age** | Eight years old |
| **Skill factor** | Some skill needed |
| **Special requirements** | Pen and paper if a running score is to be kept |

## Aim
To score points by capturing cards from the layout by matching them with cards from the hand.

## Cards
The standard pack of 52 cards is used.

## Preparation
Any player may pick up the cards, cut them, and deal them one at a time face up to each player clockwise until a Jack appears; the player to whom it is dealt becomes the first dealer.

The dealer shuffles the pack, the player to his right cuts and the dealer deals clockwise face down as follows: with two players, twelve cards each; three players eight cards each; four players, six cards each. The next four cards are placed face up in a square to the centre of the table. There shouldn't be more than two of the same rank among them. If there are three (or four) of the same rank insert those in excess of two back in the pack and replace with the next card or cards. The remaining cards are placed face down in a pile in the centre of the square to form the stock (see illustration on p23).

## Play
Each player takes up his cards, and beginning with the 'eldest hand' (the player to the dealer's left) takes turns to play. The object is to capture from the layout certain cards which score points. These cards are:

i) All red cards. 'Plain' cards from 2 to 8 score points according to their pip value. Red 9, 10, J, Q, K each score ten points. A red Ace scores 20 points.

ii) With three or four players only, ♠A scores 30 points.

iii) With four players only, ♣A scores 40 points.

A player captures a card from the layout by playing to it a card from his hand which makes the pip total of the two cards ten. Thus an Ace captures a 9, and vice versa, a 4 captures a 6 and vice versa, a 5 captures another 5. A 10, Jack, Queen or King can be captured only by playing a card of exactly equal rank to it, eg a Jack captures a Jack, and so on. Only one capture can be made on each turn.

A player making a capture takes both cards (the card from the layout and the card he played to it) and places them face down before him. A player who cannot, or who declines to make a capture (he might prefer not to use a black 10 to capture another black 10, hoping to take a red 10 with it later) must play one of his cards face up to the table. Thus a player's hand diminishes by one card on each turn.

A player's turn is always concluded, whether he captured or not, by his turning face up the top card of the stock. If it should be of a rank which can capture one of the cards in the layout, then it captures that card and the player adds the two cards face down to his captured pile. Otherwise the turned-up card from stock is added to the remaining cards in the layout, and the turn ends. If the game is played without mistakes, the last card from the stock will always match the last card in the layout and the table will be cleared, with all 52 cards distributed among the players' win piles.

**Scoring** At the end of the game, each player takes up the cards he has captured and calculates the number of points he has won according to the point-scoring list above. Notice that black cards do not score any points with the exception of the ♠A, which is a scoring card when three or four play, and the ♣A, which is a scoring card only when four play. The total points at stake per game are: 210 (two players), 240 (three players), 280 (four players). The player with most points is the winner. If a series of games is required, with a running score kept with pen and paper, then each player should deal an agreed number of times, say twice each.

**Example hand**
The illustration opposite shows a game in progress between three players. Each player has had two turns, and therefore their original hands have been reduced to six cards each. All three have made captures, and the cards they have won are in face-down piles beside them.

It is Player A's turn to play. All he can do is capture ♣6 with ♣4, which will not score any points. Once he has done this he turns the top card over from stock. If it is an Ace, King or 8 he can capture another card from the layout, and his turn ends. If it is not an Ace, King or 8, he adds the card face up to the layout and again his turn ends. In either case his hand will be reduced to five cards and it is Player B's turn. Provided Player A has not had the luck to find a King on top of the stock Player B will capture ♥K with ♦K and contribute 20 points towards his final score. Player C will be hoping that the ♦9 remains in the layout until it is his turn, as he will be able to capture it with ♠A and thus improve his eventual score by 40 points.

Stock

Player A

Player B

Player C

Player A's captures

Player B's captures

Player C's captures

# Clock

Clock is a good patience game for a child learning to tell the time. It is a game very rarely got out, and depends entirely on chance, but a child should turn up at least one card for each number on the dial, which may be sufficient to please.

| | |
|---|---|
| **Alternative names** | Sundial, Travellers |
| **Players** | One |
| **Minimum age** | Six years old |
| **Skill factor** | No skill needed |
| **Special requirements** | None |

**Aim**
To end with every card turned face up in piles by rank, laid out in the form of a clock face.

**Preparation**
A large playing area is needed. The cards are shuffled and dealt to a 'tableau' in the form of a clock face: twelve packets of four cards are dealt face down to positions representing the twelve numbers on the dial. It does not matter whether the cards are dealt one at a time to each position in turn, or in batches of four. A final packet of four is placed in the centre of the clock face.

**Play**
Play begins with the top card of the centre packet being turned over and placed face up on the outside of the packet on the clock face which represents the number of the rank of the card. For example, a 3 of any suit would be placed face up outside the packet at the three o'clock position on the dial. An Ace represents 1 o'clock, a Jack 11 o'clock and a Queen 12 o'clock. A King which is turned up is placed face up next to the packet in the centre.

When a card has been played to its spot on the dial or the centre, the top card is taken from the face-down packet in that position and played in turn to its appropriate position, with a card being taken from there and played to its spot, and so on.

The game ends in failure if the fourth King appears before all the numbers on the clock face are filled with face-up cards, because when the fourth King appears and is played to the middle there are no more face-down cards there with which to carry on the game. The game is won if every card gets turned face up (ie, if the final card to be turned face up is the fourth King).

**Example game**
The illustration shows a game in progress. Every spot on the dial has had at least one card played to it.

The last card to be played was the ♠3, and the player takes the top face-down card from the pile at 3 o'clock and plays it to its position, taking the next card from there, and so on.

# Commerce

Commerce is a modern version of an old French game called Brelan de Famille which was popular throughout Europe. It has similarities to Thirty-One. It was at one time a gambling game, but is now played mainly as a family game.

| | |
|---|---|
| **Alternative names** | Trade or Barter (see Variants) |
| **Players** | Three to twelve |
| **Minimum age** | Eight years old |
| **Skill factor** | Some judgement needed |
| **Special requirements** | Three counters per player |

## Aim
To hold the best three-card hand and thus win the pool.

## Cards
The standard pack of 52 cards is used, the cards ranking from Ace (high) to 2 (low), although in sequences Ace can also count low.

## Preparation
Any player can pick up the cards, shuffle, and begin to deal cards face up one at a time to all players clockwise to his left. The first player to be dealt a Jack becomes the first dealer. Thereafter the deal passes to the left.

## Play
Each player puts a counter into a pool in the centre. The dealer shuffles, the player on his right cuts, and the dealer deals the cards one at a time face down to each player including himself and one to a 'widow' (an extra hand), until all players and the widow hold three cards.

The widow is turned face up on the table. Before he looks at his own cards, the dealer has the option of exchanging his whole hand for the widow.

No other player has the option to exchange his whole hand for the widow, but beginning with the 'eldest hand' (the player to the dealer's left) each player in turn has the opportunity to exchange one card in his hand with one from the widow (which may be a card which a previous player has put into the widow by exchanging).

On his turn, a player who is satisfied with his hand, whether he has exchanged a card or not, knocks on the table and play ends. All the players' hands are compared and the player with the highest ranking hand wins.

Hands are ranked as follows:

i) 'Triplets', or three cards of the same rank. Three Aces rank highest, then three Kings and so on down to three 2s.

ii) 'Sequences', or three cards of the same suit in sequence. The highest sequence is A, K, Q, then K, Q, J and so on down to 3, 2, A. Note that Ace can be the top card of the highest sequence or the bottom card of the lowest.

iii) 'Point', which is the total points value of two or three cards of the same suit, with Aces counting eleven; Kings, Queens and Jacks counting ten each; and other cards counting their pip value. Among hands of equal point, one containing three cards of the same suit beats one containing two cards.

If two or more players hold hands which tie for best, the winner is the dealer, if he is involved, otherwise the player nearest to his left. The winner collects the pool, and the deal passes. Players drop out when they lose all their counters. The player who at the end wins all the counters is the winner.

At the end of a game with many starters, the last two players might get into a long drawn-out end game with more than 20 counters between them. To prevent this it is suggested that when two players are left a player who gets two-thirds of the total counters in circulation is the winner.

## Variants

**Trade or Barter** This is a version of the game (often itself called Commerce) which has the following differences:

i) Each player receives three more counters than there are players.

ii) There is no widow.

iii) A player on his turn may exchange one of his cards by one of two methods:

  a) He may 'trade', which involves buying a new card from the dealer, who gives him the top card of the undealt pile. The card rejected remains face down on the table. The player pays the dealer one counter for his new card, and the counter belongs to the dealer, not the pool.

  b) He may 'barter', which involves passing a card face down to the player on his left, who may accept it, in which case he then has the same options, or he may reject it, which he does by knocking on the table, bringing the deal to a halt.

iv) If the dealer does not win, he gives the winner one counter. However if the dealer's hand is of the same class as the winner (ie both have a triplet, sequence or a point) the dealer must give one counter to each of the other players. This is the reason why players must have more than the three counters of the parent game.

As with the parent game, the winner of the hand takes the pool, and a player who runs out of counters leaves the game. If a player has to leave the game because, as the dealer, he is forced to give all other players one counter and does not have enough counters, he gives the winner one counter and distributes the remainder to the other players to his left as far as they will go.

The winner is the player who ends with all the counters, but, as suggested above, to prevent a drawn-out struggle between the last two of many players, the winner might be decided by the first to accumulate two-thirds of the total counters in circulation.

**Example hand**
Six players hold the hands as illustrated.

|  |  |  |
|---|---|---|
| Player A | Player B | Player C |
| Player D | Player E | Player F |

Player A is the first to play and passed ♥J face down to Player B, hoping to get a club in exchange. Player B accepts ♥J but passes ♥6 back. Player B passes ♠10 to Player C and gets ♥A in exchange. This gives Player B a point of 21, as his hand is now ♥A, J, ♦J. (Notice that if he'd kept his ♥6 he would have a point of 27.) Player C passed the dangerous ♥A, hoping to get a diamond, whereupon he would have knocked with a three-card point of at least 19. However Player B knocks with his point of 21 and collects the pool.

Player F, who was the dealer, and who holds the same class of hand as the winner, but has a point of only nine, has to pay one counter to each of the other players.

In both Commerce and Trade or Barter, a point of 20 or more is often enough to win the pool, especially if a player holding it knocks early on, before other players have had a chance to exchange cards.

# Crazy Eights

Crazy Eights is a simple gambling game. It is unrelated to another game
called Crazy Eights which is a version of Switch. If children are involved
it can be played for counters.

| | |
|---|---|
| **Alternative names** | None |
| **Players** | Two to eight; four to eight is best |
| **Minimum age** | Seven years old |
| **Skill factor** | No skill needed |
| **Special requirements** | Cash, chips or counters for staking; a bowl or saucer to hold the pool of stakes |

## Aim
To play all your cards to the centre.

## Cards
The standard pack of 52 cards is used. The ranking of the cards is immaterial, but
for settlement purposes cards have the following points values: Aces 15, court
cards 10, other cards their pip value.

## Preparation
The value of the stake must be agreed.

Any player may pick up the cards, shuffle and begin to deal cards one at a time
to each player round the table until a Jack appears. The player dealt the Jack
becomes the first dealer. The deal then rotates clockwise.

Each player puts a stake of two units into the centre to form a pool. The dealer
shuffles, the player to his right cuts, and the dealer deals five cards face down
to each player, including himself, one at a time. He then lays out the next eight
cards face up to the centre in two rows of four, and puts the rest to one side. It
doesn't matter if ranks are duplicated.

## Play
Beginning with the 'eldest hand' (the player to the dealer's left), each player in
turn may lay one card only from his hand face up to a card in the centre matching
it in rank. As play progresses, more than one player may play a card to the same
card in the centre. A player who cannot match a card in his hand with one in the
centre passes.

**Settlement** Should a player get rid of all his cards, he shouts 'Crazy Eights' and
collects the whole pool.

Should the game end without any player being able to get rid of his cards, each
player counts the total value of the cards in his hand, based on the scale already

given. Half the pool goes to the player with the highest count, and half to the player with the lowest. If two or more share for highest or lowest, their half of the pool is divided between them, with any units over being left in the pool for the next game.

**Example hand**

In the illustration, no player managed to scoop the pool of twelve units. The scores were as follows:

| | |
|---|---|
| Player A | 15 (two cards left) |
| Player B | 12 (two cards left) |
| Player C | 23 (four cards left) |
| Player D | 2 (one card left) |
| Player E | 21 (three cards left) |
| Player F | 2 (one card left) |

Thus Player C took six units for highest, and Player D and Player F took three units each for joint lowest.

# Cribbage

According to John Aubrey's *Brief Lives*, Cribbage was invented by Sir John Suckling (1609–42), and this is widely accepted, with the proviso that he developed it from an earlier game called Noddy. Although elements of it are found elsewhere, as a whole it is quite unlike other modern games.

Cribbage has changed little since its invention nearly 400 years ago, the main change being that in the 19th century the number of cards in each hand when dealt changed from the original five to six. Although five-card Cribbage is still played, the six-card version is so predominant that it is described here, with the five-card version outlined under Variants.

Cribbage was originally for two players and, although it has been adapted for three or four, the two-handed version is described as the parent game, as it is one of the best card games for two players. It is nowadays often called Crib.

| | |
|---|---|
| **Alternative names** | Crib |
| **Players** | Two; three and four for Variants |
| **Minimum age** | Twelve years old |
| **Skill factor** | A skilful game |
| **Special requirements** | A Cribbage or Noddy board for scoring, or pen and paper |

## Aim
To be the first to reach a score of 121.

## Cards
The standard pack of 52 cards is used, the cards ranking from King (high) to Ace (low).

## Preparation
Cards are cut, and the player cutting the lower card deals. He shuffles and the non-dealer cuts. The dealer deals six cards to each player, beginning with the non-dealer, one at a time, face down. The remainder of the pack is put to one side, face down, for the moment. The deal alternates with each hand.

## Play
Each player examines his cards and each 'lays off' two cards face down to form a central pile of four called the 'crib' or, more commonly, the 'box'. The box is a third hand which in the second part of play, called the 'show', belongs to the dealer.

After laying off, the non-dealer cuts the pack and the dealer turns over the top card of the lower half and places it face up on the top of the reunited pack. This card is known as the 'start'. If it is a Jack, the dealer immediately scores two points (announced as 'two for his heels').

**Pegging** In the first part of the game cards have a value: court cards count ten, and other cards their pip value, with Ace counting as one. The score is usually kept on a Cribbage board, also called a Noddy board, which contains two groups of 60 holes, one on each side, with a central hole at each end, as illustrated below. Each player keeps his score with the use of two pegs. The first time he scores he puts a peg in the relevant hole, the second time he takes the second peg and advances it the required number of holes ahead of the first, and so on, with at each score the second peg leap-frogging the first. The game is to 121 points, ie twice round the board and into the end hole. Scoring is thus called 'pegging'.

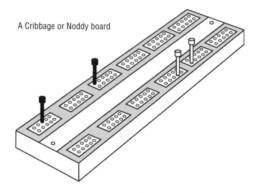

A Cribbage or Noddy board

The hands are now played out. The non-dealer lays his first card and announces its value (as given above). Players do not combine their cards as they will need them later. The dealer then plays a card announcing the cumulative score (the combined value of the cards played) and so on. The cumulative score cannot exceed 31. If a player cannot lay a card which will keep the score at 31 or below, he says 'Go' or 'No'. The other player then continues on his own, until he has played all his cards or he, too, cannot play a card which will not bring the cumulative score to 31 or below. A player cannot say 'No' if he can play a card legitimately, ie a card which will not take the total past 31. The last player to play a card pegs one (announced as 'last for one'), or if he brings the total to exactly 31 he pegs two (announced as '31 for two'). If either player has cards left they play a second round of pegging, beginning with the player who did not play the final card in the first round.

During the pegging, certain combinations also allow a player to peg as follows:

*Fifteen*        A player who brings the cumulative score to 15 pegs two (announced as 'fifteen two').

| | |
|---|---|
| *Pair* | A player who plays a card of a rank his opponent has played pegs two (announced as 'Two for a pair', and also announcing the cumulative total; for example, if the cards laid had been 3, 6, 6 he would announce 'Fifteen two and two for a pair'). |
| *Pair-royal* | If a player can play a third consecutive card of the same rank, he pegs six. To follow on with the example, if he played another six after the 3, 6, 6 he would announce 'Pair-royal for six, total 21'. Of course, in most games he might not be so formal as this, and might say 'And another for six, making 21'. |
| *Double pair-royal* | If a player laid a fourth card of the same rank as the previous three (rare, but not unheard of) he pegs twelve, announcing, to follow the same example 'Double pair-royal for twelve, making 27', but would more likely say, with a touch of triumph 'And another 6 for twelve, total now 27'. |

It should be noted that, although all court cards have a value of ten, only cards of the same rank, such as two Jacks or two Kings, count as a pair. It is impossible to score a double pair-royal with cards of a rank above 7 as the cumulative score would exceed 31.

| | |
|---|---|
| *Run or sequence* | During the pegging a player who plays a card which makes a run with the two or more played before it, pegs one for each card it contains. Suits are irrelevant, as is the order of the cards played. Thus if the first three cards played are 2, 4, 3, the player who played the 3 pegs (and announces) 'three for a run'. If the next person plays 2, he, too, will peg three for a run (now comprising 4, 3, 2) and if the next player plays 5 he will peg four for a run (comprising 4, 3, 2, 5). A run cannot, of course, have two cards of the same rank within it, so while 6, 5, 7 is a run, adding another 5 to make 6, 5, 7, 5 does not achieve a run. |

It is possible to score for a run or any other combination, and two points for bringing the cumulative total to 15 or 31, at the same time. For example, if the first three cards played are 4, 6, 5 the layer of the 5 pegs five – three for the run and two for 'fifteen'.

**Show** After the pegging, the players pick up their cards and score again for the show.

The non-dealer pegs first, and then the dealer pegs for his hand and then for his crib. For the show, the start is combined with the hand, making in effect a hand of five cards, although there is no need to move the start from its position on top of the pack. Points are scored for combinations as follows:

| | |
|---|---|
| *Fifteen* | For each combination of two or more cards which total fifteen a player pegs two. |
| *Pair* | For each pair a player pegs two (note that this covers pairs-royal and double pairs-royal, since, for example, if a player holds three cards of the same rank three different pairs can be made from them). |

| | |
|---|---|
| *Run* | For each run of three or more cards a player pegs the number of cards in the run. |
| *Flush* | For four cards of the same suit a player pegs four. If the start is also of the same suit he pegs five. However, a flush in the crib is not scored unless the start is also of the same suit, when the dealer scores five. |
| *His nob* | If a player holds the Jack of the same suit as the start, he scores 'one for his nob'. |

Cards can be used more than once in one or more combinations. Every possible combination is scored. The illustration shows two hands, A and B, with the start.

Hand A          Start          Hand B

Cribbage players lay their hands on the table and count their hands out loud.

For Hand A, the player would say 'Fifteen two, fifteen four, fifteen six, fifteen eight, two for the pair is ten and one for his nob eleven' (formed from ♦J, ♥2, ♠3, then ♣K, ♥2, ♠3, then ♦J, ♦2, ♠3, then ♣K, ♦2, ♠3, then ♥2, ♦2 and finally ♦J of the same suit as the start).

For Hand B, he would say 'Fifteen two, fifteen four, fifteen six, fifteen eight, two for the pair is ten and six for runs is 16' (formed from ♥7, ♥8, then ♣7, ♥8, then ♦2, ♠6, ♥7, then ♦2, ♠6, ♣7, then ♥7, ♣7, then ♠6, ♥7, ♥8 and finally ♠6, ♣7, ♥8).

Counting the hands aloud allows the opponent to count as well and check the score. If the scorer misses a combination and claims too few points, there is a convention by which his opponent can say 'Muggins' and count the overlooked points for himself, but friendly players need not play this rule and can allow the overlooked points to be scored. When meeting a new opponent, however, one should check if the 'Muggins' rule is in operation.

The highest score which can be achieved with one hand at the show is 29. The hand is J, 5, 5, 5, with the start the fourth 5, of the same suit as the Jack in the hand. This scores 16 for fifteens and 12 for the double pair-royal, plus one for his nob. All other scores up to 29 can be achieved except 19, 25, 26 and 27; sometimes players who score nothing claim a score of 19 as a joke.

**Scoring** As explained above, a game is to 121 points. On each deal the scores are taken in this order: his heels, the pegging, the non-dealer's hand in the show, the dealer's hand, the crib hand. Once a player has reached 121, it is customary not to finish the hand.

If a player fails to reach 61 before his opponent pegs 121, he is said to be 'lurched' and has lost the equivalent of two games, but this is only relevant if playing for money.

## Example hand

Suppose the dealer deals to the non-dealer the following first hand: ♣K ♥Q ♠J ♣6 ♠6 ♣5. To himself he deals ♠10 ♣9 ♥4 ♣3 ♠3 ♥2.

The non-dealer will put his pair of 6s into the crib. These are dangerous cards to give to the dealer in his crib, but it leaves him with an excellent hand himself, with plenty of opportunities for it to be improved by the start: any court card or 5 would be excellent.

The dealer will put ♠10 and ♣9 into his crib. They might form a run for him and keeping his small cards gives him six for runs which another 2, 3, or 4 would more than double. The start is turned up and is the ♦J. The dealer immediately pegs two for his heels.

The hands are shown below.

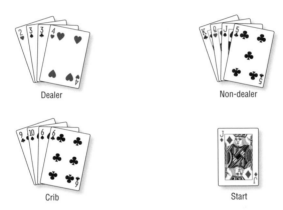

Dealer  Non-dealer

Crib  Start

The non-dealer leads ♣K (announcing 'ten'), the dealer plays ♣3 (13). The dealer knows that if the non-dealer plays a 2 for 'fifteen two', he can make a run with ♥4 and even if then the non-dealer makes a run also, he himself can make another. However, the non-dealer plays ♥Q (23). The dealer plays ♥4 (27), the non-dealer says 'Go' and the dealer plays ♠3 for 30 and pegs one for last.

The non-dealer now leads ♠J to begin another round, the dealer plays ♥2 (12) and the non-dealer plays ♣5 (17) to peg one for last.

So far the dealer has pegged three and the non-dealer one.

The non-dealer now scores his hand in the show. He has eight for fifteens, two for a pair and six for runs, pegging 16. The dealer has four for fifteens, two for a pair and six for runs, pegging twelve. The dealer now takes his crib, which is surprisingly good. He has four for fifteens, two for a pair and three for a run, pegging nine. So the dealer has so far pegged 24 and the non-dealer 17. The non-dealer now takes the cards and shuffles in preparation for the next hand.

## Variants

**Five-card Cribbage** Many players think the traditional game, in which the two hands are of five cards only, is a more skilful game. The differences from the above are as follows.

Each hand is dealt five cards only. Each player lays away two cards to the crib, which thus consists of four cards, while the players' hands are reduced to three.

In the pegging stage, when 31 is reached, or when neither player can play a card, the pegging ends, irrespective of whether either or both players still have cards in their hands or not. A second round of pegging is not started, as it is in six-card Cribbage.

The game is to 61 points (once round the Cribbage board). Because of the smaller hands, scoring is slower than in six-card Cribbage.

The advantage of having the crib first is greater in five-card Cribbage than in six-card Cribbage, and to compensate the non-dealer pegs three points at the beginning of the game for 'last'. When six-card Cribbage became more popular, this convention was dropped.

In the show, a flush, of course, counts as only three, since the hand is of only three cards, but it counts four with the start. A flush in the crib counts only if it includes the start, when it counts five.

The strategy of five-card Cribbage is different. Because the hands are smaller in the show, they cannot score as many points, so the pegging gains in importance, as does laying away to the crib. The crib, with its extra card, often scores more than the hands. The dealer, therefore, in laying away, might favour putting his more promising cards into the crib, while the non-dealer, in laying away, will concentrate on 'baulking' the crib for the dealer, ie laying away cards from which it is difficult to make runs or fifteens, and trying to keep cards which would be useful in pegging. Five-card Cribbage, because of the way a high-scoring crib can affect the score, is a game in which fortunes can fluctuate quickly.

**Seven-card Cribbage** Some players like seven-card Cribbage, although it is far less popular than the other variants. It is played in the same manner as the six-card game with the following differences: seven cards are dealt to each hand, of which two are laid off to the crib. The hands thus consist of five cards and the crib four. It is possible to have four rounds of pegging. In the show a flush scores five, or six with the start (one point per card). A flush in the crib scores five, since it must match the start. Game is to 181 points.

**Three-handed Cribbage** Three players each play for themselves. The deal passes to the left, as does the turn to play. Players are dealt five cards each, and the dealer deals one card face down to the table to begin the crib. Each player lays off one card to the crib, which thereby consists of four cards. Play is as in the six-card game. In the pegging, when 31 is reached, or when no player can go further, the player to the left of the player who played the last card leads to the next round. At the show, the hands are scored in the order of the 'eldest hand' (the player to the dealer's left), the player to his left, the dealer, crib. Game is to 61.

There are Cribbage boards for three players; they are either triangular, or the usual board contains an arm which folds away when two play, but swings out for three. They are also rare, so scoring is usually by pen and paper.

**Four-handed Cribbage** Four people play, in two partnerships of two. Partners are determined by all drawing from a spread pack, the two highest playing the two lowest. Partners sit opposite each other. The drawer of the lowest card is first to be the dealer.

The eldest hand cuts for the start, and leads. Play passes to the left, and proceeds as in six-card Cribbage described above. A Cribbage board is adequate for scoring, as partners' scores are combined. At the show, scores are taken in turn, from the eldest hand round to the dealer, who last of all pegs for his crib.

# Cucumber

Cucumber is basically a gambling game but, with its attractive name and simple rules, it is a game which can be enjoyed by children as well as adults. It is a Swedish game played in countries around the Baltic Sea.

| | |
|---|---|
| **Alternative names** | Gurka, Ogorek |
| **Players** | Two to eight |
| **Minimum age** | Eight years old |
| **Skill factor** | Some skill needed |
| **Special requirements** | Pen and paper for scoring |

## Aim

To avoid being caught with the highest ranked card when each player's hand is reduced to one card.

## Cards

The standard pack of 52 cards is used, the cards ranking from Ace (high) to 2 (low).

## Preparation

Any player may pick up the cards, shuffle and deal them to his left face up one at a time until a Jack appears. The player dealt the Jack becomes the first dealer. The deal subsequently passes to the left.

The dealer shuffles, the player to his right cuts, and the dealer deals the cards clockwise one at a time face up to all players including himself until all have six cards.

## Play

The 'eldest hand' (the player to the dealer's left) leads any card to the table to begin a trick. Each other player in turn, if able, must play a card equal to, or higher in rank than, the previous card played. Aces count high. Suits are irrelevant. A player who cannot play a card high enough to equal or beat the previous card must play the lowest card he has. It is important that he plays his lowest, since the object is not to be stuck with the highest card on the last round, and this is the manner by which players are forced to play their lowest cards.

When each player has played, the player who played the highest card in the trick takes the trick and leads to the next. If two or more cards in a trick are equal highest, the player who played the last of the equal cards takes the trick.

When five tricks have been played, each player has one card left, which he reveals face up on the table. The player with the highest card (or all those who tie for highest) collects penalty points according to the value of the card: Ace counting 14, King 13, Queen 12, Jack 11 and the other cards at their pip value.

Each player's penalty points are noted on a scoresheet, and when a player's total reaches 30 he is 'cucumbered', and drops out of the game.

The last player remaining is the winner.

**Strategy** It is not always best to play your highest card. Sometimes an Ace kept for the fourth or fifth rounds means that on these rounds a player will always have a high card to play to protect himself from having to play his smallest. Player A in the example game which follows used this technique and was never forced to play his lowest card, thus keeping the lowest card he was dealt, ♦6, for the showdown. It was still joint highest card at the end, but he could not have played better.

**Example hand**

| Player A | Player B | Player C |
| Player D | Player E | |

Five very different hands are dealt as in the illustration. Player A is to lead and chooses ♣J. Play proceeds as follows:

| | *Player A* | *Player B* | *Player C* | *Player D* | *Player E* |
|---|---|---|---|---|---|
| 1 | ♣J | ♠K | ♦3 | ♠10 | ♦10 |
| 2 | ♦Q | ♣8 | ♥8 | ♠Q | ♠2 |
| 3 | ♣9 | ♣A | ♦5 | ♠6 | ♦9 |
| 4 | ♥A | ♥5 | ♦8 | ♣2 | ♥4 |
| 5 | ♠A | ♣3 | ♠7 | ♦2 | ♠4 |

Players now reveal the cards they are left with as follows:

| ♦6 | ♣5 | ♥6 | ♠5 | ♥3 |
|---|---|---|---|---|

Players A and C are equal highest and receive six penalty points each.

# Demon

Demon and Klondike (see p61) are the best-known games of patience. Both are often called Canfield in the UK and the USA, although the name is properly attached only to Demon. This is because it was said to have been invented by a famous US gambler and casino owner of the 19th and early 20th centuries, William A. Canfield, who would 'sell' the pack to a punter for $52 ($1 per card) and pay out $5 for each card in the foundation row at the end of the game. While a player can frequently obtain the eleven cards necessary in the foundation row to make a profit from Mr Canfield, it is a difficult game to get out entirely.

| | |
|---|---|
| **Alternative names** | Canfield, Thirteen |
| **Players** | One |
| **Minimum age** | Eight years old |
| **Skill factor** | No skill needed |
| **Special requirements** | None |

## Aim
To end with four piles of cards, one for each suit, in sequence.

## Preparation
Thirteen cards are dealt face down in a pile, and the top card of the pile is turned face up. This pile is known as the 'heel'. The next four cards are dealt face up in a row to the right of the heel to form the 'tableau'. The next card is dealt face up above the first card of the tableau. This is the first 'foundation' card, and decides the rank of all the other foundation cards. The remaining cards form the stock.

## Play
The other three cards of the foundation rank should be played in a row to the right of the first foundation card as they become available. These cards will be built up in suit and ascending sequence until all the cards in the pack are built on the foundations. The sequence is 'round-the-corner', ie Queen, King, Ace, 2, 3 and so on.

The exposed cards on the heel and the bottoms of the columns of the tableau are all available to play. Once all available moves have been made, the stock is taken face down in hand and turned over in bundles of three, without disturbing their order, to a waste pile, or 'talon'. The top card of the talon is now also available to play to the foundations or tableau. Cards are played to the tableau in columns in descending order of rank and in opposite colours, for example ♥4 or ♦4 may be played on ♠5 or ♣5. These sequences are also round-the-corner, so if an Ace is at the foot of a column, a King of the opposite colour can be played to it.

A whole column in the tableau may be transferred to another provided the sequence is maintained, for example a column headed by ♥8 or ♦8 can be transferred to a column ending with a ♠9 or ♣9. An emptied tableau column is filled immediately by the top card of the heel, the next card in the heel then being turned face up. If the heel becomes exhausted, an empty column is filled by an exposed card from the talon, but this need not be done immediately – one may wait until a more useful card is exposed.

When the whole stock has been played to the talon (the last bundle may be of only one or two cards), and all possible moves have been completed, the talon is picked up and turned over without rearrangement and is again played to the table as before in bundles of three. The game ends in success when all cards are built to the foundations; in failure when the whole stock has been played to the talon without it being possible to play a card to tableau or foundation.

### Example game
The heel, foundation card and tableau are dealt as illustrated.

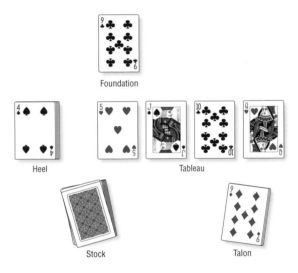

Foundation

Heel

Tableau

Stock

Talon

The play then begins with the ♠4 being built from the heel onto the ♥5, and the next card of the heel being faced. The ♣10 is then built on to the ♣9 in the foundation row and is replaced by the second card of the heel, the third card then being faced. The ♠J is built onto the ♥Q and its place in the tableau filled by the next card from the heel. The cards played from the heel may themselves offer chances to build further.

When all activity is over, the stock is taken in hand and the first bundle of three cards played to the table to begin the talon, as shown. The first card exposed is the ♦9, which being a foundation card is played to the foundation row to the right of the ♣9, and the ♦10 and then later diamonds are played to it as they become available. If the card in the talon exposed by the moving of the ♦9 will fit into the tableau or foundation row, it is moved there. If not, the next bundle of three cards is turned from the stock onto the talon, and any possible moves made, and so on.

## Variants

A popular variant to this game is that instead of dealing a card to the foundation row to determine the rank of the foundations, the foundations are always the Aces (as they are in many patience games). Only eleven cards are dealt to the heel, and the top card is not faced. The heel is used only to supply a card to a column in the tableau which becomes empty, and only then is the card turned face up. Aces are played to the foundation row as they are exposed (either in the original four cards to the tableau, or as the top card in the waste pile, or as the card turned up from the heel to fill a gap in the tableau).

# Fan Tan

Fan Tan is this game's usual name, despite the fact it is popular with children and Fan Tan is also the name of a notorious Chinese gambling game in which punters bet on how many beans will remain in a pile from which they are being removed four at a time, and usually lose, often suspiciously.

| | |
|---|---|
| **Alternative names** | Card Dominoes, Domino, Parliament, Sevens, Spoof Sevens |
| **Players** | Three to eight |
| **Minimum age** | Eight years old |
| **Skill factor** | Skill is needed to play well |
| **Special requirements** | None, but cash, chips or counters if played for stakes |

## Aim
To get rid of all your cards by playing them to the table.

## Cards
The standard pack of 52 cards is used, the cards ranking from King (high) to Ace (low).

## Preparation
Any player may shuffle the pack and deal the cards clockwise, beginning with the player to his left, one at a time face up, until a Jack appears. The player dealt the Jack becomes the dealer for the game. He shuffles and the player to his right cuts. If the game is played for stakes, each player puts one unit into the pool. Since the whole pack is dealt, some players might get one more card than others. In this case some prefer that those players with one card short put an extra unit into the pool. Others ignore it, as the deal rotates to the left anyway.

The dealer deals the cards clockwise to his left, one at a time face down until the whole pack is exhausted.

## Play
The 'eldest hand' (the player to the dealer's left) plays first, and must lay a 7 to the table. If he cannot, he passes and the next player must play a 7 if he can, and so on until a 7 is laid. When a 7 is laid a player on his turn can lay the 6 or the 8 of the same suit to one side of it. From then on a player on his turn can add to the sequence at either end, down to the Ace or up to the King, or lay another 7.

In this way the four suits get built up in rows from Ace to King. Only one card may be played at a time, and a player must go on his turn if he can. It is not permitted to hold up the development of a row by passing when one could play a card. A player who can play more than one card can choose which to play.

A player who cannot play a card passes, and if the game is being played for stakes he adds a unit to the pool. The first player to get rid of all his cards wins the pool. The other players, if the game is being played for stakes, add a unit to the pool for each card left in their hands.

The game is one enjoyed by children, and can of course be played without stakes, the winner being the player who plays all his cards to the table first.

**Example hand**

Fan Tan is a game which repays good judgement in the playing of the cards. At the beginning a player will usually have a choice of cards to play. His danger cards are Kings and Aces, and to a lesser extent Queens and 2s, because he cannot play these until other players have played the intermediate cards from the 7 towards the end of the sequence. So the player should try to play cards which get the sequences moving towards the ends where he holds the danger cards.

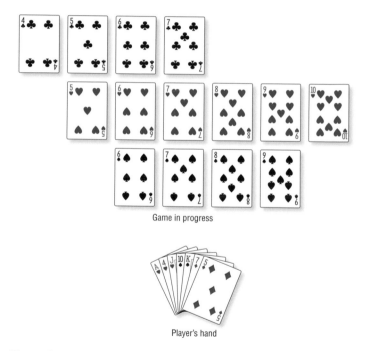

Game in progress

Player's hand

The illustration shows a layout soon after the start of a game, when 14 cards have been played, plus the hand of the player whose turn it is. He is in a strong position, because he holds four of the seven cards which can be played to the layout. He has the heart suit blocked, one end of the spade suit and also has the ♦7, so nobody can play a diamond until he lays it. He should hold back the ♦7 for as long as he can. The threats to his winning are the ♥A and the ♠K. He should play either the ♥4 or the ♠10, followed by the other on his next turn. By the turn after that, he might be able to get rid of the ♠K or ♥A, while everybody else still holds diamonds. In fact, he has an excellent chance of winning, if, as they say, he plays his cards right.

# Farmer

Farmer is a game that originated in France and became very popular in the United States. It is a simple gambling game of the same type as Pontoon, and Pontoon players might like to try it for a change.

| | |
|---|---|
| **Alternative names** | The Farm |
| **Players** | Three to twelve; about six to eight is best |
| **Minimum age** | Eight years old |
| **Skill factor** | Some judgement needed |
| **Special requirements** | Cash, chips or counters for staking |

### Aim
To build a hand of 16 points or as near to 16 as possible without exceeding 16.

### Cards
From a standard pack are removed all the 8s and all the 6s except ♥6, making a pack of 45 cards. The cards have points values as follows: each Ace counts one, each court card ten, and all other cards are their pip values.

### Preparation
Any player may pick up the cards, shuffle and deal them round face up to his left one at a time until a Jack appears. The player dealt the Jack becomes the first dealer, or 'farmer'. Unless playing for money, counters are shared out equally among the players.

### Play
The farmer puts as many chips or counters as there are players into a pool (the farm). The other players all contribute one chip.

The farmer then shuffles the cards, the player to his right cuts and the farmer deals one card face down to each player, excluding himself. The farmer is in effect the 'banker' for the game.

The players look at their cards without exposing them. Beginning with the 'eldest hand' (the player immediately to his left), the farmer deals with each player in turn. Each player must accept one more card from the farmer, face down from the top of the pack. The player may then decide to stand or take another and may continue to take extra cards as long as he wishes. The cards are dealt face down.

The object of each player is to get a hand with a count as close as possible to 16 without exceeding it. Should a player's count exceed 16, he 'busts' and obviously draws no further cards, but he must not announce that he has 'busted' and he must leave his cards face down upon the table. Only at the end of the deal may any player reveal his hand.

When the farmer has dealt with each player, the players expose their hands. All who have busted must pay the farmer one chip for each point that they have exceeded 16. Note that this is paid to the farmer, and not to the farm, or pool.

Of the remainder, a player who has a points total of exactly 16 takes the whole pool and becomes the new farmer and starts a new game. The pool cannot be divided, so if two or more players exceed 16, the winner is:

i)  the player who in his count of 16 holds the ♥6; if none holds ♥6 then

ii) the player to make 16 with the fewest cards; if equal, then

iii) the player with 16 nearest to the farmer's left

If no player has 16, the farmer keeps the farm for the next deal, but the player whose score is nearest to 16 collects one chip from the other players who did not exceed 16. If there is a tie, the winner is decided by the same method as given above.

The cards are collected up, the farmer (new or old) shuffles, the player to his right cuts and a new deal takes place.

**Example hand**

| Player A | Player B | Player C | Player D | Player E | Player F |

Player A is dealt ♥7 and draws ♦J. He has exceeded 16 and draws no more.

Player B is dealt ♣9 and draws ♦5 and stands with a count of 14.

Player C is dealt ♥K and draws ♣A and stands with a count of 11.

Player D is dealt ♠3, draws ♦4 and thinks it worth drawing another, since even if he draws a ten-count card he will lose only one chip to the farmer. He draws ♦Q and busts.

Player E is dealt ♥6 and draws ♠4. It is annoying for a player to get the coveted ♥6 but not a ten-count card with it to complete a count of 16. Perhaps because of this he ignores the advice given under Strategy below and draws a further card. He gets ♥4 and stands with a count of 14.

Player F is dealt ♦K and draws ♥J busting and ending his turn.

All players now expose their hands. Three players busted. Player A pays one chip to the farmer, Player D pays one chip to the farmer and Player F pays four chips to the farmer. Profit to the farmer: six chips.

Players B and E each have a count of 14. Player E wins because he holds the ♥6. If he hadn't, Player B would have won as he holds the fewer cards. So Players B and C each pay one chip to Player E.

**Strategy** This is a game where caution is likely to succeed better than optimism. A player would be unwise to draw with 5, 4 (a count of nine) for example, hoping to draw a 7 for a count of 16, or improving with a smaller card. His chance of drawing a 7 are about 10 to 1 against, but his chance of drawing a card to take his score past 16 is little better than even; to be precise 23–20 against. With a count of nine he is unlikely to win, but it is not impossible (it depends on the number of players) but he cannot lose more than one chip, while drawing another card will more often than not result in a loss, which is likely to be of three chips. The percentage play is not to draw with a total higher than eight.

### Variants

Descriptions of this game tend not to agree with each other. The way the first farmer is decided, and how the farm changes hands, are the main matters of disagreement, and the methods given above are invented for this book to solve the dilemma.

The traditional way of deciding the first farmer, or banker, is by 'auction'. The player who bids most becomes the farmer and he puts into the farm, or pool, not the one chip per player as recommended, but the number of chips which he bid. However, when the farm is won by a player with a 16 count, the number of chips he must put in the new farm is vague. To be fair he should put in the same number as the original farmer, which is more than he or any of the other players thought the farm was worth (or they would have bid higher). Logically therefore, a player should be allowed to refuse the farm, which detracts from the game. One description of the game states that a player who wins the farm takes the pool but does not automatically become the new farmer. Instead the farm is auctioned again. This is fair, but the same player is likely to bid highest each time, so the farm might never change hands, which is boring.

Another variation to be found is that instead of a player who busts (exceeds 16) paying the farmer the number of chips corresponding to the number by which he bust, he pays one chip only. This is a big advantage to the player as opposed to the farmer, as it limits a player's possible losses on any deal to one chip. He need not then be cautious (as advocated under Strategy above), but can draw towards 16. The farmer will not collect more than one chip per player (although more players will bust as they attempt to get 16). Also the farm will tend to change hands at shorter intervals as players hit 16 more often, and the farm will not be as valuable as before. But the main objection to this variation is that on every deal only one chip changes direction at a time among players and between players and farmer, thus reducing the variety of the game's outcomes.

Another variation allows the farmer to be a player as well, and to deal himself a hand. This is very much in favour of the farmer. He has no fear of busting, as he pays any penalty chips for doing so to himself. Therefore he can throw caution to the winds and draw extra cards at will.

None of the variations in this section are therefore recommended.

# Fifty-One

Fifty-One is one variation of the many adding-up games popular in central Europe. Jubilee, Obstacle Race and Twenty-Nine are others included in this book.

| | |
|---|---|
| **Alternative names** | None |
| **Players** | Two to five |
| **Minimum age** | Seven years old |
| **Skill factor** | Little skill needed |
| **Special requirements** | None |

## Aim

To avoid taking a progressive communal pip count above the number 50, and thus avoid being eliminated from the game.

## Cards

A 32-card pack is required, and is formed by stripping a standard pack of the ranks 2 to 6. The remaining cards each have a value according to rank, as follows:

| A | 1 | 10 | -1 |
|---|---|----|----|
| K | 4 | 9 | 0 |
| Q | 3 | 8 | 8 |
| J | 2 | 7 | 7 |

Notice that a 10 counts as minus 1 and a 9 counts as zero.

## Preparation

A first dealer is chosen by any player dealing the shortened pack around one at a time face up to all players until a Jack appears. The player dealt the Jack becomes the first dealer, the deal thereafter passing to the left. The dealer shuffles the cards and deals cards to each player clockwise one at a time according to the number of players as follows:

With five players, five cards each

With four players, six cards each

With three players, eight cards each

With two players, ten cards each

He then places the remainder of the pack face down in a pile in the centre, turning the top card face up. This card becomes the starter.

Fifty-One

## Play

Players take their cards in hand and, beginning with the 'eldest hand' (the player to the dealer's left) each player adds a card to the pile in the centre, announcing as they do so the running total of all the cards played, including the starter, according to the values of each card as set out above.

The object is to avoid bringing the total above 50. When a player is forced to bring the total to 51 or more, he brings the deal to an end and is eliminated, and so on.

The deal passes, the cards shuffled, and the remaining players are each dealt fresh cards (the number of cards per player corresponding to the number of players left, as listed on p49). Play takes place as before until another player is eliminated. The last player remaining is the winner. If all players get rid of their cards before the total of 51 is reached, they all go through to the next round.

## Example hand

| | Player A | Player B | Player C |
| --- | --- | --- | --- |
| | Player D | Starter | Player E |

Five hands are dealt as in the illustration, with the starter being ♥J. Player A has to play first and chooses ♥8. The play proceeds as follows, with the players announcing the totals:

| | Player A | Player B | Player C | Player D | Player E |
| --- | --- | --- | --- | --- | --- |
| 1 | ♥8 (10) | ♦Q (13) | ♦K (17) | ♣K (21) | ♣8 (29) |
| 2 | ♠7 (36) | ♥Q (39) | ♠K (43) | ♠Q (46) | ♣Q (49) |
| 3 | ♣10 (48) | ♦J (50) | ♠9 (50) | ♦9 (50) | ♠10 (49) |

Player A, with ♣7 and ♥K in his hand, now must take the total past 50, and so is eliminated. As it would have been Player A's turn to deal next, Player B becomes the new dealer and a second round begins.

50

# Go Fish

Go Fish is practically the same game as Authors, a proprietary card game of Victorian times, in which special cards contained quotations from famous authors, the object of the players being to collect sets of quotations. It was thought to be educational. Go Fish and the modern game Authors are slightly different versions of the game, both played with the normal pack of cards. The games are so alike that often one of them will appear in books under the name of the other, and if both appear in the same book the headings seem to be interchangeable. It is therefore best to look on them as the same game. The version here is the one best suited to younger children, with a variant for slightly older players.

| | |
|---:|:---|
| **Alternative names** | Authors (see Variants), Fish |
| **Players** | Two to six |
| **Minimum age** | Six years old |
| **Skill factor** | Some skill needed |
| **Special requirements** | None |

## Aim
To collect sets of four cards of the same rank.

## Cards
The standard pack of 52 cards is used. The rank of the cards is immaterial.

## Preparation
The pack is spread face down and each player takes a card. The player with the highest card (Ace high, 2 low) is the first dealer. Thereafter the deal passes to the left. If there are two players, the dealer deals each seven cards, one at a time alternately. With three or more players, each player is dealt five cards. The remainder of the pack is placed face down in the centre to form the stock.

## Play
Beginning with the player at the dealer's left, each player in turn may ask any other player to hand over all the cards he holds of a certain rank; for example, he might say to a specific player 'give me your Kings' or 'have you any Kings?'. A player must hold a card in the rank that he is asking for; he cannot, for example, ask another player for Kings unless he himself holds a King. A player asked for cards must hand over all the cards he holds of that rank, even if it be three. If the asking player is successful, and is handed a card or cards, he has another turn, and may continue to ask whichever player he likes for cards (remembering that he has to hold at least one card of that rank himself), provided he continues to be successful.

Should the player asked not hold any cards in the rank specified, he says 'Go fish' or 'Fish'. The asking player must then take the top card of the stock into his hand. If he is lucky enough to draw a card of the rank he asked for, he can show it and his turn continues. Otherwise his turn ends and the next player (to his left) takes a turn to ask.

If a player succeeds in getting four cards of the same rank he lays them face up in front of him on the table.

If during the course of play a player runs out of cards, through laying a set on the table or by being forced to hand them to another player, he may draw the top card of the stock when his turn comes round, but he may not use it to ask another player for a card until the following turn (by when, such is the cruelty of the game, he may have had to relinquish it, and be out of cards again).

When the stock is exhausted, play continues with each player asking for cards in turn, but of course being unable to draw if unsuccessful. A player who runs out of cards when the stock is exhausted must remain idle until the game ends.

The game will end when all 13 sets of cards are on the table, and the winner is the player who has most.

### Variants

**Authors** This version of the game is here called Authors, though not all card games writers would agree. It is more skilful, and the minimum age is more like nine or ten years. Even then it is best when played by children of much the same age, who therefore have similar skill in remembering which players hold which cards. Some adults play this game for stakes.

There are two main differences to Go Fish as described above. First, all the cards are dealt, meaning that some will get one more than others. It follows that there is not a stock from which to draw, and if a player does not get the card he asked for, his turn ends.

The second difference is that on his turn a player asks for a single specific card, naming suit and rank; for example he may ask a specific player 'have you the Queen of clubs?' He must hold in his hand a card of the rank of the card he asked for but of a different suit – in other words he cannot ask for a card he already holds.

A player gaining four of a kind must lay them on the table immediately.

It will be seen that a set has to be built gradually, and one cannot gain one by getting three cards all at once (unless he separately asks for three cards, naming the suit each time). Thus a player who can remember where the cards are has a big advantage.

Some players allow a player to ask for a card he already holds. It adds deception and more skill to a game. For example, if Player A holds ♥3 and ♣3, and asks and gets from another player ♠3, he has another turn, and must try to find the ♦3. If he fails, the player holding the ♦3 can, on his turn, ask Player A for ♠3, knowing he has it. He knows Player A has at least one other 3 too, so having been passed ♠3, he might ask him for ♣3. Having acquired this, he must now try Player A or another player for ♥3. If he goes for Player A again he will have the set.

On the other hand, supposing on getting the ♠3, Player A had asked for the ♥3, a card which he holds. He will obviously fail to get it. The player holding ♦3, on his turn, will assume that Player A holds ♠3 (because he saw him take it) and ♣3 (since he must hold another 3 to ask for ♠3) but will assume that Player A doesn't hold ♥3, since he asked for it. So he might ask Player A for ♠3 and ♣3, but then try another for ♥3. He will fail of course and, on his turn, Player A will be able to pick up all the missing 3s to complete his set.

This variant adds another element to the game and is recommended.

Go Fish

# Golf

There are forms of Golf patience games for golf addicts, none really satisfactorily simulating the game of golf. This competitive game's somewhat forced likeness to golf is merely that it is played over nine deals, or 'holes'. It is a rummy-type game.

| | |
|---|---|
| **Alternative names** | None |
| **Players** | Two to six |
| **Minimum age** | Eleven years old |
| **Skill factor** | Good judgement needed |
| **Special requirements** | Pen and paper for scoring |

## Aim

To collect four cards with as low a pip total as possible and record the lowest cumulative score over nine deals.

## Cards

The standard pack of 52 cards is used. Cards have point values as follows: 2 to 10 have their pip value, Jack and Queen count ten each, King counts zero and Ace counts one.

## Preparation

The pack is spread face down and each player draws a card, the drawer of the highest being the first dealer. For this purpose, cards rank Ace (high) to 2 (low), and, if there is a tie for highest, those tying draw again. The deal thereafter passes to the left. The dealer deals four cards to each player face down in the form of a square. The top card of the remainder is dealt face up to the centre to begin a discard pile, the remaining cards being placed beside it face down to form the stock.

## Play

Each player may look at the two cards in his square which are nearest to him, but must replace them face down on the table and not look at them again, ie he must remember their values. He may not look at his other two cards at any time.

Beginning with the 'eldest hand' (the player to the dealer's left) each player in turn clockwise may do any of the following:

i) Take the top card of the discard pile and exchange it with one of his four cards, placing the rejected card face up on the discard pile and the new card face down in its place.

ii) Look at the top card of the stock, and either reject it by placing it immediately on the discard pile, or exchange it with one of his four cards in the manner described above.

Rummy players will notice that the principles of changing a card in the hand for a new one are exactly the same as in Rummy.

When, and if, a player exchanges his two unknown face down cards, he will know the value of each of his four cards. However they remain face down.

The object is to obtain as low a count with the four cards as possible, each rank having a value as stated above. When a player has a total count which he thinks may be the lowest, or close to lowest, he may bring the deal to an end on his turn by 'knocking' (ie tapping the table) instead of drawing a card from the discard pile or stock. Each other player in turn has one more opportunity to draw and discard before play ends.

Each player then turns over his four cards and his total count is debited against him on the scoresheet. After nine deals the player with the lowest cumulative total is the winner.

If the stock runs out during a deal, the discard pile is turned over to form a new stock.

**Strategy** The decision when to knock is always a finely balanced one. For example, a player whose two known cards are Kings and/or Aces might consider knocking immediately since, with two medium cards as his unknown pair, and thus a score of around 12, he might well be lowest (the average score of four cards is 23, the average per card being 5.77). Generally speaking a player will want to change his two unknown cards before considering knocking, in case they are cards of a high count.

Unknown cards     Stock     Discard pile

Known cards

PLAYER'S HAND

The illustration shows the sort of choice a player is frequently faced with. Assume it is early in the game. The player's known cards are ♥2 and ♣8 (in practice, of course, they will be face down on the table). Should he exchange the ♣8 for the ♦5, thus certainly reducing his count by three? Or should he take the opportunity of replacing one of his unknown cards with the ♦5, which is just below the average count? The card he rejected might well be lower than the ♦5, of course. Or should he turn over the top card of the stock and give himself another decision? As well as decisions to make like this, the player must also note what cards other players might be discarding and consider how close they might be to knocking. It is an interesting game.

# Gops

Gops is a game of memory, calculation and bluff, in which the players each know the opponent's cards. It can be said therefore to be a game of skill alone, especially when two play, and indeed the name Gops is thought to come from the initials of Game of Pure Strategy.

| | |
|---|---|
| **Alternative names** | None |
| **Players** | Two or three; two is better |
| **Minimum age** | Twelve years old |
| **Skill factor** | A skilful game |
| **Special requirements** | None |

## Aim
To win as many points as possible by capturing cards in the diamond suit.

## Cards
When two play, the standard pack minus the heart suit is required; when three play, the whole pack is required.

## Preparation
The pack must be separated into its four suits. When two play, one player has the spade suit and the other the club suit, while the heart suit is set aside as not required. When three play, the third player has the heart suit. In both cases the diamond suit is the suit to be fought for. One player thoroughly shuffles the diamond suit, and another cuts it. It is then placed face down in the centre of the table. There is no deal, as the cards are shared suit by suit as described.

## Play
The object is to win as many points as possible by winning the diamonds, each of which has a value: Ace counts one point, 2 to 10 each count the number of their pips, Jack counts eleven, Queen twelve and King thirteen. There are therefore 91 points at stake.

Play commences with the top card of the diamond pile being turned face up. This is the first card to be played for. Each player then selects a card from his hand and places it face down upon the table. When both (or all three with three players) cards are laid down, the players turn them over and the player who played the higher (or highest) card wins the trick. The cards (as the diamonds) rank from Ace (low) to King (high). The winner takes the diamond, placing it face up to his right. Each player then places the card he played to the trick to his left, also face up.

Thus throughout the game, all the diamonds that have been won, and all the cards that have been played to tricks, can be seen by all players. When the first diamond has been won, the second card in the diamond pile is turned face up, and played for in the same manner, and so on until all 13 diamonds have been won, which coincides with each player having played all his cards.

In the two-handed game, if both players turn over the same value card on any trick, the diamond played for is not won, but set beside the diamond pile. The next diamond is turned up, and the winner of that takes both diamonds. If there are two successive ties, then three diamonds are played for on the next trick, and so on.

If there is a two-way tie in the three-handed game, the diamond is set aside as before, and the next diamond turned over. This is won, as usual, by the highest card played to the next trick, but the previous diamond can only be won by the higher card of the two played by the players who previously tied for it, the third player having already lost in his bid for it.

If the last diamond or diamonds turned over are tied for, each player having exhausted his hand, they are not won by any player.

The player winning the most points in diamonds, using the values set out above, is the winner.

**Strategy** The skill lies in winning tricks by the narrowest margin, eg by beating an 8 with a 9. Conversely to lose an 8 to a 9 is a waste, as you could have lost by playing an Ace, thus conserving your 8. It is usually not worth laying a King to win, say, the ♦3. Clearly, when the ♦K is the top card, you want to win the 13 points it carries, but it would be fatal to play a high card, say a Queen, in an attempt to win it, if you should lose to an opponent's King.

It might pay sometimes to bluff. For example, if a medium size diamond appears which you think your opponent will play high to win, you could play an Ace and let him win it, knowing that your hand is now stronger than his and you could recoup later. On the other hand, if he is one fond of playing an Ace to bluff you, you could try to anticipate when he will do it, and win the diamond with a 2. It is all a question of psychology.

### Example hand
In a three-handed game, Player A has clubs, Player B has spades and Player C has hearts. The play might go as follows:

| | Diamond turned | Player A | Player B | Player C |
|---|---|---|---|---|
| 1 | ♦4 | ♣2 | ♠3 | ♥2 |
| 2 | ♦5 | ♣5 | ♠A | ♥5 |
| 3 | ♦9 | ♣K | ♠2 | ♥J |

On trick 2, Players A and C tied, so ♦5 was placed to one side to be fought for between them on the next trick. On trick 3, Player A played his King to win ♦9 and ♦5 (14 points) while Player C played Jack, a bad error. Player B, who could not win the ♦5, played ♠2, letting the other two fight it out, and now has much the strongest hand, while Player C is struggling.

| 4 | ♦ 10 | ♣ A | ♠ 4 | ♥ K |
|---|------|-----|-----|-----|

Player C played his King to ensure winning ten points, but again it was not good for him, as he only beat two low cards (♥6 would have been enough).

| 5 | ♦ 8 | ♣ 3 | ♠ 8 | ♥ 9 |
|---|------|-----|-----|-----|
| 6 | ♦ J | ♣ 4 | ♠ Q | ♥ A |
| 7 | ♦ Q | ♣ 6 | ♠ 9 | ♥ Q |
| 8 | ♦ 2 | ♣ 7 | ♠ 5 | ♥ 3 |
| 9 | ♦ 7 | ♣ 8 | ♠ 10 | ♥ 4 |
| 10 | ♦ K | ♣ 9 | ♠ K | ♥ 6 |
| 11 | ♦ 6 | ♣ Q | ♠ 6 | ♥ 7 |

Player A realizes that ♦6 is the highest diamond left and he decides to be sure of it with his ♣Q.

| 12 | ♦ A | ♣ 10 | ♠ J | ♥ 8 |
|----|------|------|-----|-----|
| 13 | ♦ 3 | ♣ J | ♠ 7 | ♥ 10 |

All players could have played better, and perhaps the trick of bluffing was overdone at times, but Player B, lucky to win with ♠3 on the first trick, did well to play low on the next three tricks and eventually triumphed. The final scores were Player A 25 points, Player B 36 points and Player C 30 points. Had Player C played ♥6 on trick 4, and won, he might well have won the whole game.

# Jubilee

Jubilee comes from the Czech Republic. It is a simple game requiring that players can add and subtract numbers up to 15 from totals up to 200 plus. A little skill is required to avoid setting up easy scores for opponents.

| | |
|---|---|
| **Alternative names** | None |
| **Players** | Two to seven; perhaps best for three |
| **Minimum age** | Eight years old |
| **Skill factor** | Some skill needed |
| **Special requirements** | Pen and paper for scoring |

## Aim
To score points by making a cumulative pip total of cards played reach a number divisible by 25.

## Cards
A 61-card pack is made up from two standard packs by including two complete spade suits, one complete suit of hearts, two sets of Ace to nine in clubs (ie all the clubs without the 10s and court cards) and four Jokers. The diamond suits are not required.

## Preparation
From the face-down 61-card pack each player draws a card and the drawer of the highest card (Ace high, 2 low, Joker zero) becomes the first dealer. A second draw is required for any who tie for highest.

## Play
The dealer shuffles, the player to his right cuts, and the dealer deals eight cards to each player one at a time face down, the remaining cards being placed face down in a pile in the centre to form a stock.

The 'eldest hand' (the player to the dealer's left) begins the play by laying a black card to the table, taking the top card from stock into his hand. He announces the value of the card he played. The cards have the following values: Aces 15 points, court cards (K, Q, J) ten points, other cards their pip values, with Jokers counting zero. The black cards (spades and clubs) count plus these amounts, and the hearts count minus these amounts.

After the first card is played, each player in turn clockwise adds a card to it and announces a new running total of all the cards played. He cannot take the score below zero. He also takes a card from stock, so that until the stock is exhausted, each player's hand remains at eight cards.

The object is to make the total a multiple of 25 (ie 25, 50, 75, 100 etc). These are called 'jubilee' numbers and score ten points for the player who makes them. If the number is also a multiple of 100 (ie 100, 200) then the score for it is doubled to 20 points. These numbers can be made either forwards with a black card or backwards with a red card. However, if a player is forced to play a card which jumps a jubilee number (either forwards or backwards), he loses five points. If a player makes and scores for a jubilee, the following player or players can play a Joker and also score for a jubilee, as the total remains the same.

When the stock is exhausted, players play out their last eight cards, when, if nobody has made a mistake in adding or subtracting, the final total of the pile should be 217. The total scores of the players will vary according to how many jubilees have been made. The player with most points is the winner.

# Klondike

Klondike is a widely played patience game, perhaps the most widely played of all. It is often misnamed Canfield, which is really the name by which Demon is known in the USA, or sometimes simply Patience.

| | |
|---|---|
| **Alternative names** | Canfield (mistakenly), Fascination, Triangle |
| **Players** | One |
| **Minimum age** | Eight years old |
| **Skill factor** | No skill needed |
| **Special requirements** | None |

## Aim
To end with four piles of cards, one for each suit, in sequence from Ace up to King.

## Preparation
The cards are shuffled and seven cards are dealt face down in a row. Six face-down cards are then dealt in a row underneath but one card to the right, each overlapping a card in the row above. Further rows, each shorter than the previous, are added until the 'tableau' is completed, and the first card in each row is turned face up, as shown in the illustration overleaf. The four blank spaces are the 'foundations' where the Aces will go when they become available. The cards not dealt form the stock.

## Play
The cards available for play are those exposed at the foot of each of the columns, and they can be built to a foundation, or can be packed on each other in descending sequences of alternate colours. Cards can be packed from one column to another in units, for example a ♦7, ♣6 exposed at the foot of a column can be transferred as a whole to a ♣8 or ♠8 exposed at the foot of another column. Aces should be played to the foundations as soon as they become available.

When a card or group of cards is transferred from a column, the bottom card of the column is turned over and becomes available. If a column is emptied, it can be filled only by an available King, either with other cards attached to it in sequence, or alone.

When all the cards in the tableau have been played as far as possible, the stock is taken into the hand, and the top card is turned over and is available for play. If it cannot be played to the tableau or the foundations it is placed face up on the table to begin a waste-pile, or 'talon'. The card at the top of the talon is always available for play.

If the turned-over stock card can be played, all other moves which then become possible in the tableau can be made, including those resulting from the exposure of new cards at the foot of the columns. When all possible moves have been made, the next card is turned over from the stock to the talon, and so on.

It is not obligatory to play a card to its foundation immediately, but once it is built there it cannot be moved back into the tableau. The stock is turned over once only, ie there is no redeal. The game is won if all the foundations are built up to the Kings.

**Example game**

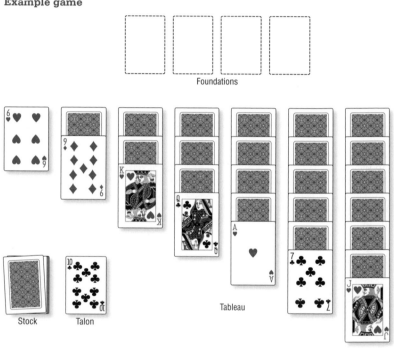

Foundations

Stock    Talon

Tableau

In the illustration, the ♥A is moved to a foundation, and the card below it faced; the ♥6 is packed on the ♣7; the ♥K is moved to fill the column from which the ♥6 was taken; the ♣Q is packed on the ♥K, followed by the ♥J; with each time the face-down card which finds itself at the foot of a column turned face up.

The first card turned from stock to begin the talon is the ♣10, but this can immediately be packed on ♥J, and the ♦9 can then be packed on to it.

# Knaves

Knaves is said to have been invented by the late Hubert Phillips who, as well as being a writer on card games, was a humorous columnist of a national newspaper and a panellist on the BBC's *Round Britain Quiz*. He slightly immodestly described Knaves in one of his books as 'a good game for three'. It is based on an old game called Polignac. The Knave is the old name for the card which is now more usually called the Jack.

| | |
|---|---|
| **Alternative names** | Jacks |
| **Players** | Three |
| **Minimum age** | Ten years old |
| **Skill factor** | Some skill needed |
| **Special requirements** | Pen and paper for scoring |

## Aim
To win as many tricks as possible to reach a total of 20 points, while avoiding taking tricks containing any of the four Jacks, which are penalty cards.

## Cards
The standard pack of 52 cards is used, the cards ranking from Ace (high) to 2 (low).

## Preparation
Each player draws a card from the spread pack, the drawer of the highest card being the first dealer.

The dealer deals 17 cards to each player clockwise one at a time, beginning with the player to his left. The final card is turned face up to denote the trump suit. The deal passes to the left with each hand.

## Play
The 'eldest hand' (the player to the dealer's left) leads to the first trick, and subsequently the winner of a trick leads to the next; see p155 for an explanation of tricks and trick-taking. The normal rules of trick-taking apply: players must follow suit to the card led if able, and may trump or discard if unable. The highest trump in a trick wins it, and if there are none the highest card of the suit led wins it.

The object is to win tricks, as each trick won scores a point. However, each Jack taken in a trick costs a point or more. To take the ♥J costs a player four points, the ♦J three points, the ♣J two points and the ♠J one point. Each deal therefore has seven points at stake (unless a Jack is turned up as the trump card): 17 for winning tricks, minus ten to be picked up in penalties. A game is to 20 points.

### Example hand

North, East and West are dealt the hands shown below, with the ♣3 turned up as the trump card.

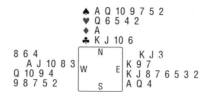

```
                    ♠ A Q 10 9 7 5 2
                    ♥ Q 6 5 4 2
                    ♦ A
                    ♣ K J 10 6
   8 6 4           ┌─────────┐       K J 3
   A J 10 8 3      │    N    │       K 9 7
   Q 10 9 4    W   │         │   E   K J 8 7 6 5 3 2
   9 8 7 5 2        │    S    │       A Q 4
                    └─────────┘
```

West is on lead. The play proceeds as follows:

| | West | North | East |
|---|---|---|---|
| 1 | ♦ 10 | ♦ A | ♦ J |

An unpleasant surprise for North on the first round!

| | West | North | East |
|---|---|---|---|
| 2 | ♥ 10 | ♥ 6 | ♥ 9 |
| 3 | ♠ 8 | ♠ 10 | ♠ K |
| 4 | ♦ Q | ♣ 6 | ♦ 3 |
| 5 | ♠ 6 | ♠ 9 | ♠ 3 |
| 6 | ♠ 4 | ♠ 7 | ♠ J |

East is forced into taking ♠J. He decides a small trump might be his safest lead at the moment.

| | West | North | East |
|---|---|---|---|
| 7 | ♣ 2 | ♣ 10 | ♣ 4 |
| 8 | ♥ 8 | ♥ 5 | ♥ 7 |
| 9 | ♣ 5 | ♣ K | ♣ A |
| 10 | ♦ 9 | ♠ 5 | ♦ 2 |
| 11 | ♦ 4 | ♠ 2 | ♦ K |

East is in trouble. A diamond lead will almost certainly get him the ♥J, as will the lead of the ♥K, and ♣Q will get him ♣J. He must make ♣Q anyway, as it is the master trump. He decides to lead his diamonds, and see what happens.

| | West | North | East |
|---|---|---|---|
| 12 | ♥ J | ♥ 4 | ♦ 8 |
| 13 | ♣ 7 | ♥ 2 | ♦ 7 |

| 14 | ♥3 | ♥Q | <u>♥K</u> |
|----|----|----|----|
| 15 | <u>♣8</u> | ♠Q | ♦6 |
| 16 | ♥A | ♠A | <u>♣Q</u> |
| 17 | <u>♣9</u> | <u>♣J</u> | ♦5 |

So West won five tricks and took no Jacks for a score of five. North took five tricks but took the Jacks of diamonds and clubs, for penalties of five points, so ending with zero. East took seven tricks, but these included the Jacks of hearts and spades, which took five points away, leaving him with two points.

At trick 16 North was helpless as the cards lay. He was sure to make ♣J whichever card he played. His only hope was that West held ♣Q, but he was unlucky.

# Knockout Whist

Knockout Whist is only related to Whist in that it is a trick-taking game. It is very simple, and is often the game used to introduce children to the trick-taking principle.

| | |
|---:|:---|
| **Alternative names** | None |
| **Players** | Three to seven |
| **Minimum age** | Eight years old |
| **Skill factor** | No skill needed |
| **Special requirements** | None |

## Aim
To win at least one trick in each round in order to stay in the game.

## Cards
The standard pack of 52 cards is used, the cards ranking from Ace (high) to 2 (low).

## Preparation
One player picks up the cards and begins dealing them, one to each player, until a Jack appears. The player dealt the Jack is the first dealer. The dealer shuffles, and the player to his right cuts.

The dealer deals seven cards to each player, one at a time, clockwise from his left. The remainder of the pack is placed face down in the centre and the top card turned face up to denote the trump suit.

## Play
The 'eldest hand' (the player to the dealer's left) leads to the first trick. The usual rules of trick-taking apply; see p155 for an explanation of tricks and trick-taking. Players must follow the suit led if they can, and if unable to follow may trump or discard. A trick is won by the highest trump it contains, or if there is none, the highest card of the suit led.

When all seven tricks have been played, any player who has failed to win a trick drops out and must wait for the next game to rejoin the action.

The player who won the most tricks deals the next round (if there is a tie, the players must draw cards from the pack to determine the dealer; highest deals). The dealer on this and on subsequent rounds chooses the trump suit after looking at his hand, and the eldest hand leads. On the second round each player is dealt six cards.

The procedure is repeated as for the first round – any player who fails to win a trick is eliminated. The third round is of five cards each, the next of four, and so on until all players but one are eliminated, which must eventually happen as the last round, if reached, is of one card each.

The winner is, of course, the last player to survive.

### Variants

Some people play that, instead of the first player who fails to win a trick dropping out, he receives a 'dog's chance' or 'dog's life'. This player is dealt a single card on the next round, and can choose to play it in whichever of the tricks he chooses. If he does not wish to play in the trick he knocks on the table when it would be his turn, including when it would normally be his turn to lead. He must play his card in at least one of the tricks in the round.

If the player wins a trick with his single card, he survives, receives a normal hand in the next round and is treated henceforth as a normal player. If he again fails to take a trick he drops out of the game in the usual way.

Just one dog's chance is available in a game, although if two or more players fail to win a trick in the same round each receives a chance in the next. Otherwise, once a player has been given a dog's chance, players who fail to win a trick in a subsequent round must drop out in the usual way.

A further variant for players who employ the dog's chance allows that if a player on a dog's chance loses again, he gains a 'blind dog's chance' in the next round. This is a single card dealt face down that may not be looked at by the player but which can be played in any of the round's tricks, as described above.

# Linger Longer

Linger Longer is a simple trick-taking game which is good for introducing younger members of the family to the function of trumps.

| | |
|---|---|
| **Alternative names** | Sift Smoke |
| **Players** | Three to six; four to six is best |
| **Minimum age** | Eleven years old |
| **Skill factor** | Some skill needed |
| **Special requirements** | None |

## Aim
To be the last player with any cards left.

## Cards
The standard pack of 52 cards is used, the cards ranking from Ace (high) to 2 (low).

## Preparation
The cards are shuffled and spread out face down and each player draws a card. The drawer of the highest card (Ace high, 2 low) becomes the first dealer. If there is a tie for highest, those who tie draw again.

## Play
The dealer shuffles, the player to his right cuts, and the dealer then deals cards one at a time face down to each player clockwise to the following amounts: with three players, ten cards each; with four players, nine cards each; with five players, eight cards each; with six players, seven cards each.

When the dealer gives himself his last card, he turns it over and shows it to the other players before taking it into his hand. The suit of this card becomes trumps.

Linger Longer is a trick-taking game, and the 'eldest hand' (the player to the dealer's left) leads to the first trick. He plays any card he wishes, and each player in turn adds a card to make up the trick. Normal rules of trick-taking apply; see p155 for an explanation of tricks and trick-taking. Each player, if able, must play a card of the suit led. If unable to, he may play a trump, or discard, ie play a card of one of the other suits. The trick is won by the highest card it contains of the trump suit or, if no trumps have been played, by the highest card of the suit led.

The winner of the trick collects up the cards and places them face down to one side. There is no value in the trick itself, but the winner of it takes the top card of the stock before leading to the next trick. The winner of the trick always leads to the next.

The object of the game is to be the last player to have any cards in his hand. That is to say that to win, a player must attempt to win as many tricks as possible, since every time he loses a trick his hand diminishes by one. A player who runs out of cards drops out of the game.

The winner is the player who has a card or cards in his hand when all others have lost theirs.

### Example hand

| Player A | Player B | Player C | Player D | Stock |

Towards the end of a game, four players are left in, three with two cards each and one with one, as shown in the illustration. Diamonds are trumps, Player A won the last trick, and leads to the next. The play continues as follows (the card in brackets indicates the card the winner of the trick picked up from the stock).

| | Player A | Player B | Player C | Player D |
|---|---|---|---|---|
| 1 | ♣Q | ♣9 | ♦2 (♥8) | ♥10 |

Player A leads ♣Q, which Player C trumps. Player D is eliminated. Player C draws ♥8, while the other two players have one card each.

| | Player A | Player B | Player C | Player D |
|---|---|---|---|---|
| 2 | ♥2 | ♠K (♣3) | ♠10 | - |

Player C chose to lead the higher of his two cards, the ♠10. Unfortunately, he chose the wrong card. Had he led ♥8, he would have won the trick and the game. But Player B wins with ♠K, and draws ♣3. Player A is eliminated with no cards left. Players B and C have one card each and Player B is forced to lead his ♣3.

| | Player A | Player B | Player C | Player D |
|---|---|---|---|---|
| 3 | - | ♣3 | ♥8 | - |

The ♣3 wins, and Player B wins the game since, although he and Player C have played their last cards, Player B, by virtue of winning the last trick, takes the top card of the stock.

### Variants

Descriptions of this game vary widely as to the number of cards dealt to each player. Some versions state that the number of cards dealt to each player should be equal to the number of players taking part, but this seems illogical. The numbers suggested above are recommended.

# Menagerie

Menagerie is a silly and noisy game for children, preferably of similar ages. If some children are older than others, a method of handicapping the elders is suggested under Variants. It is advisable that a parent supervises, as there will be disputes, and all might end in tears.

| | |
|---:|:---|
| **Alternative names** | Animals, Animal Noises (see Variants) |
| **Players** | Three or more; the more the better |
| **Minimum age** | Seven years old |
| **Skill factor** | Older children will beat younger |
| **Special requirements** | None |

## Aim
To win the majority of the cards.

## Cards
The standard pack is required for up to six players. For seven or more two complete packs shuffled together is better.

## Preparation
All players think of an animal. Each must have a different animal. For reasons which will become clear, your chances of winning are improved the longer and more complicated the name of the animal you choose. Thus hippopotamus, rhinoceros, even boa constrictor are good names to choose. This is where a supervisor might intervene in the standard rules and choose more easily pronounced names himself, putting them into a hat and letting each child pick one. Each child should keep the slip of paper with his or her animal written on it so arguments can be settled promptly. When each player has the name of an animal there is an interval, because every player has to memorize not only his own animal but that of each of the other players.

## Play
Any player may deal out the cards one at a time face down to each player until the pack is exhausted. It does not matter if some players have one more card than others. The players do not look at their cards but put them in a neat pile face down before them.

The 'eldest hand' (the player to the dealer's left) begins play by turning over the top card of his pile and placing it face down on the table in front of him where all can see it. This begins his discard pile. The player to his left turns over his top card similarly, and so on round the table. As players turn over their cards, the face-up cards will build themselves into a pile, so that each player will have a pile of face-up and a pile of face-down cards before him.

Every player should be aware of the top card of his discard pile, because sooner or later another player will turn over a card to top his discard pile which will match his own in rank (suits are irrelevant in this game). As soon as the top cards of the two piles match, the owners of the matching piles race to be the first to call out the name of the other's animal three times (this is why it is an advantage to be an animal with a long name). The first to call out the other's animal three times wins his opponent's discard pile which he takes and places face down at the bottom of his face-down pile.

The player on the winner's left then continues the game by turning up the top card of his pile as normal and placing it on his discard pile.

It is essential that a player turning over his card onto his discard pile does it smoothly and naturally and without looking at its rank before the other players can see it, as doing this would obviously give him an unfair advantage.

When a player runs out of face-down cards, he simply picks up his face-up discard pile, turns it over and begins again. A player who loses all his cards, however, drops out of the game.

Traditionally the winner is the player who ends with all the cards. However, when only two players are left the game can go on for a long time, with everybody (especially those who have been knocked out) getting bored, so a way to bring the game more quickly to an end is suggested as follows: when a player gets knocked out so that only two are left the game ends there, with the cards of the last two players counted, and the one with the most cards being the winner.

### Variants

Where there are many players and especially if some are young, it is suggested that an adult supervises to rule on disputes ('I said the three names first' etc) and that some amendments could be added:

i)   The supervisor could allocate the names of the animals, and by giving the younger children those animals with the longer names improve their chances slightly.

ii)  At any time any child may ask for a recap of the animals, and each player in turn must state the name of their animal. It might be a good idea to get the players to repeat their animals periodically anyway, especially if it looks as if younger children have forgotten which other player is which animal.

**Animal Noises** Animal Noises is similar to Menagerie, with the difference that instead of repeating three times the name of the opponent's animal, players must make its noise. Therefore only animals with distinctive noises can be used, such as dog, cow, cat, where the players would call 'woof', 'moo', 'meow'. Younger players might prefer this, and it could be made easier for them by requiring them to make the noise of their own animal rather than their opponents', thus making it unnecessary for them to remember the other players' animals.

# My Ship Sails

My Ship Sails is a good game for children. Older people can enjoy it too, even if they are not card-playing enthusiasts. It requires little skill or concentration and thus is a suitable game for the whole family to play together.

| | |
|---:|:---|
| **Alternative names** | My Sow Pigg'd |
| **Players** | Three to seven |
| **Minimum age** | Seven years old |
| **Skill factor** | Little skill needed |
| **Special requirements** | None |

## Aim
To collect seven cards of the same suit.

## Cards
The standard pack of 52 cards is used.

## Preparation
The cards are shuffled and spread on the table. Each player draws one, the drawer of the highest (Ace high, 2 low) being the dealer. The dealer deals seven cards, one at a time face down to each player clockwise. The remaining cards are put to one side and not used.

## Play
The players study their cards and each passes one card face down to the player on his left. This card must not be picked up or looked at by the player to whom it is given until he himself has passed on a card to his left. When all players have taken the new card into their hands the exercise is repeated, and continues to be, so that on each round each player passes an unwanted card to his left and receives a new card from his right.

The object is to build a hand consisting of seven cards of the same suit, so each player will start to collect the suit of which he has most cards in his dealt hand, and will pass on a card of the suit in which he holds fewest.

A player who acquires seven cards of the same suit must lay them down face up on the table and announce 'My Ship Sails'. This should be done quickly since, if two players achieve a one-suited hand on the same round, the winner is the first to make the announcement.

Note that if there are more than four players, it is inevitable that at least two are collecting the same suit. This adds to the interest, although it is unfortunate for the players concerned, as by the time they suspect what is happening it is usually too late to change suits.

It is also worth noting that with three players it is possible that there may not be seven cards of the same suit among the 21 dealt – and the odds are against there being two suits of seven each – so if three play, the players should realize that a winner might be impossible, and should stop if the game appears deadlocked. They might then agree that the player with the most cards of one suit is the winner.

### Variants

A quicker game is called My Star Twinkles. It follows exactly the same rules, but the aim is the easier one of acquiring six cards of the same suit plus one odd one.

An even quicker game is called My Bee Buzzes, and requires a winning hand of five of a suit, with any two odd cards.

These variants on the parent game might be better choices for games of three players since it will always be possible for one to win.

A suggested alternative way to find a winner when two players complete a winning hand on the same round, for all versions of the game, is to decide the winner according to the number of points his hand includes, based on King counting 13, Queen 12, Jack 11 and other cards their pip value, with Ace counting one. This avoids the unsatisfactory need for players to rush to call out their success.

# Newmarket

Newmarket is a mild gambling game, the modern version of Pope Joan. It takes its name from the famous racecourse, but there are many other names for it and, wherever it is played, there are likely to be minor deviations from the description below. As a gambling game it is more popularly played among families for pennies than among serious gamblers.

| | |
|---:|:---|
| **Alternative names** | Boodle, Chicago, Michigan, Saratoga, Stops |
| **Players** | Three to eight |
| **Minimum age** | Eight years old |
| **Skill factor** | Little skill needed |
| **Special requirements** | Four cards from another pack; cash, chips or counters for staking; a bowl or saucer to hold the pool of stakes |

## Aim
To make money by getting rid of your cards, thus winning the kitty, and also to play one or more of the 'boodle' cards, thus winning the stakes placed upon them.

## Cards
The standard pack of 52 cards is used, the cards ranking from King (high) to Ace (low). Four cards from another pack are also required; a King, a Queen, a Jack and a 10, each of a different suit.

## Preparation
A unit of stake must be agreed. For this description we will assume it is one chip.

The four cards from the other pack (called 'boodle' cards) are laid out in a row upon the table, with a bowl beside them to hold the chips contributed to a kitty.

Any player may pick up the cards, shuffle and begin to deal cards one at a time to each player round the table until a Jack appears. The player dealt the Jack becomes the first dealer. The deal subsequently passes to the left.

Before the deal, each player must place five chips to the centre. One goes into the kitty, and the other four are distributed among the boodle cards as the player wishes; he may place one on each card, all four on one card, or distribute his stake in any other combination.

The illustration opposite shows a layout as it might be with five players, before the deal.

The dealer then deals the cards one at a time face down to each player and one to a spare or 'dead' hand, which is not used. It does not matter if some players receive a card more than others, as the deal rotates.

Boodle cards

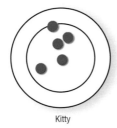

Kitty

## Play
The 'eldest hand' (the player to the dealer's left) plays face up to the table in front of him a card of whichever suit he prefers, but it must be the lowest card he holds in that suit. He announces its rank and suit. The player who holds the next higher card in that suit then plays it face up to the table in front of him and announces it in the same manner, and so on. The playing of the cards is 'stopped' either by the sequence reaching the King, or by it reaching one of the cards in the dead hand. When the sequence is stopped, the player who played the last card begins a new sequence. Like the opening leader, he may lay a card of any suit, but it must be the lowest card he holds in that suit. It may be of the same suit as was stopped, if he wishes, in which case the sequence may also be stopped by reaching the point at which the previous sequence in that suit began.

When a player lays a card matching one of the boodle cards, ie the identical card in both suit and rank, he collects the chips on that card. The first player to get rid of all his cards collects the kitty and play ends. Should any chips be left on the boodle cards, they remain there for the next deal. All players distribute five chips again as before, and the previous eldest hand becomes the dealer for the next hand.

## Variants
**Michigan** Michigan is the most popular name for the game in the USA, where the standard version varies from that described above in the following respects:

*Boodle cards* These are A, K, Q, J of different suits (ie Ace is included, not 10).

*Rank of cards*  The cards rank from Ace (high) to 2 (low).

*Staking*  The dealer places two chips on each boodle card, while the other players put one (ie there is no choice and the boodle cards are evenly staked). There is no kitty.

*Dead hand*  The cards are dealt as in Newmarket, except that cards to the spare or dead hand are dealt first rather than last, ie the dead hand is between the dealer and the eldest hand. Moreover, it is not dead, but a 'widow', which belongs to the dealer. After looking at his hand, the dealer may, if he wishes, exchange it with the widow. He is not allowed to look at the widow first, nor is he allowed to change back if he decides he prefers his original hand to the widow. Some players agree that, if the dealer is happy with his dealt hand, another player may buy the widow. Whoever offers most for it, takes it and pays the dealer for it. He may not change his mind after buying it. The original hand of the player who takes the widow is discarded face down and becomes the dead hand.

*Stopped suits*  When a suit is stopped, the player whose card stopped it must change the suit to restart play, ie he cannot begin a new sequence in the suit that was stopped. Some players restrict this even further, and the new suit must be of the opposite colour to the stopped suit. In either case, if the player due to start the new sequence does not hold a card with which he may legitimately do so, the player on his left begins the new sequence, subject to the same restrictions.

*Kitty*  In the absence of a kitty, the player who goes out collects one chip from all the other players for each card still held in their hands at the end of the play.

*General*  Although Newmarket and Michigan are basically the same game, the number of variants listed are numerous. However, neither game is always played as stated, and many players play the game with elements of one and elements of the other. It is not a question of which rules are correct, but of which the players choose to apply. All should agree before play starts, of course.

# Nomination Whist

Nomination Whist is an enjoyable trick-taking game invented in the 1930s without acquiring a universally accepted name. It has a variety of names when found in books, and the matter is further complicated by Nomination Whist also being used for another game which involves a secret nominated partner. The game described here is played without partners, secret or otherwise.

| | |
|---|---|
| **Alternative names** | Blackout, Botheration, Jungle Bridge, Oh Hell!, Oh Pshaw, Oh Well! |
| **Players** | Three to seven |
| **Minimum age** | Ten years old |
| **Skill factor** | Some skill needed |
| **Special requirements** | Pen and paper for scoring |

## Aim
To score points by correctly forecasting the number of tricks you will make on each deal.

## Cards
The standard pack of 52 cards is used, the cards ranking from Ace (high) to 2 (low).

## Preparation
Any player may pick up the cards, shuffle and begin to deal cards one at a time to each player round the table until a Jack appears. The player dealt the Jack becomes the first dealer. The deal subsequently passes to the left.

It is necessary to agree a scorer.

The dealer shuffles the cards, and the player to his right cuts. The dealer deals seven cards face down to each person, one at a time clockwise. The remaining cards are placed face down on the table and the top card is exposed to indicate the trump suit.

## Play
Beginning with the 'eldest hand' (the player to the dealer's left), each player nominates the number of tricks he intends to make, out of the potential seven in the first deal, and these are noted on the scoresheet. When it is the dealer's turn to nominate, he is not allowed to bring the total of tricks nominated to seven (this prevents the possibility that, with seven tricks nominated and seven to play for, every player will get his forecast correct).

The eldest hand leads to the first trick. The normal rules of trick-taking apply.

Players must follow suit to the card led, and if unable to may trump or discard. The trick is won by the highest trump it contains, or if it is without trumps by the highest card in the suit led; see p155 for an explanation of tricks and trick-taking. The hands are played out, and each player whose forecast was exactly correct scores ten points (to score too many tricks is as wrong as to score too few). In addition, each player scores one point for each trick he makes. The scores are noted down and a cumulative total kept for each player.

The deal passes to the left for the second round, and the process is repeated, except that each player is dealt only six cards. The number of cards dealt is reduced by one at each deal. As before, the dealer is not allowed to bring the total of tricks nominated to six, then to five, and so on.

There is one restriction on the number of tricks a player may nominate to win. Because nominating zero is often an easy option (especially when the hands are of only one or two cards), it is forbidden to bid zero more than twice running.

On the seventh round, the hands consist of one card only. On the eighth round, the hands are increased to two cards, and from then on the hands increase by one card each round until on the thirteenth round the hands are again seven cards each. After this round the game ends and the player with the highest score wins.

**Example hand**
Suppose there are seven players and it is the fourth round, in which each player holds four cards only. The seven hands are as illustrated.

Player A        Player B        Player C        Player D

Player E        Player F        Player G

Player G dealt, so Player A is the first to bid. Hearts are trumps.

Player A bids one. The only threat against him getting one is if the Ace of trumps is led and he loses his King. He is unlikely to make a trick with any other card.

Player B bids one, his main threats being that clubs are not led, or are trumped, or that having made the ♣A he has to lead another club, which also wins a trick.

Player C bids one, expecting to make either ♦A or ♠Q and hoping to be able to discard the others.

Player D bids one on the same principle, expecting to make either ♠A or ♦K, and not expecting to make both, as all three of the previous bidders have bid one. His bid of one means that all four tricks are now accounted for.

Player E knows this and is fairly confident in bidding zero.

Player F also bids zero.

Player G, the dealer, is barred from bidding zero as four tricks have already been bid. However, with two trumps and a King he might well have bid two had he been first bidder, so now he is happy to bid one, expecting, with all the other bidding, that he will lose one of his trumps, and hoping to discard his ♣K.

There are five tricks bid for, so each of those who bid one knows he has to fight for his trick. Player A, who leads, will not lead his King of trumps, in case another player holds the Ace. It would be safer for him to trump on a club lead, say. He decides to lead ♠4. Play proceeds as follows, with the number of tricks bid by each player shown in brackets:

| | Player A (1) | Player B (1) | Player C (1) | Player D (1) | Player E (0) | Player F (0) | Player G (1) |
|---|---|---|---|---|---|---|---|
| 1 | ♠4 | ♣10 | ♠Q | ♠A | ♠10 | ♠K | ♥J |

Player G plays his larger trump, as he wants only one trick. He then leads his other trump, feeling confident that somebody would over-trump. Had he kept it he might have been forced to win with it later (as the cards lay, he was right).

| | | | | | | | |
|---|---|---|---|---|---|---|---|
| 2 | ♥K | ♣5 | ♦Q | ♣7 | ♦J | ♦8 | ♥7 |
| 3 | ♠2 | ♦5 | ♣6 | ♣2 | ♠5 | ♠3 | ♣K |

Disaster for Player E. Who could have thought that with players fighting for tricks, he would win a trick with ♠5? Worse was to follow:

| | | | | | | | |
|---|---|---|---|---|---|---|---|
| 4 | ♦6 | ♣A | ♦A | ♦K | ♠6 | ♣9 | ♣3 |

So Player E, who did not want a trick, made two with ♠6, 5. Three players who nominated one trick did not make a trick at all. And none of the three Aces dealt made a trick.

Player A and Player G each score eleven points (ten for a correct forecast and one for a trick), Player F ten (for a correct forecast), Player E two (for his two tricks) and Player B, Player C and Player D nil. Each player's bid was reasonable, and all played as well as possible.

### Variants
Because the restriction on bidding zero more than twice running gets very troublesome over the run of deals when the hands are of one or two cards only, some players ignore this rule.

Some players, instead of turning up a card to indicate trumps, prefer the trump suit to be rotated, for example hearts, clubs, diamonds, spades.

# Obstacle Race

Obstacle Race is another adding-up game from central Europe, in this case Germany. It is similar to Jubilee, but the pack, obstacles and value of the cards are different. Like the other games in this book it is a good one for children to practise their adding-up skills.

| | |
|---|---|
| **Alternative names** | None |
| **Players** | Three to six |
| **Minimum age** | Seven years old |
| **Skill factor** | Some skill needed |
| **Special requirements** | Pen and paper if a running score is to be kept |

**Aim**
To bring a pile of cards to one of the pip counts which scores a point; alternatively to avoid exceeding it, which loses a point.

**Cards**
A 32-card pack is required, ie a standard pack stripped of all cards from 2 to 6.

**Preparation**
A first dealer is chosen by the shortened pack being spread face downwards and each player drawing a card, the drawer of the highest card becoming the dealer. If more than one game is played, the deal passes to the left.

**Play**
The dealer deals the cards one at a time face down to each player beginning at his left. If four play, each will get eight cards, but if three, five or six play they will get respectively ten, six or five cards each, with two left over in each case. The two left over the dealer shows to the other players and places in a pile face up to the centre of the table announcing their combined value, according to the following scale:

| Card | Value | Card | Value |
|---|---|---|---|
| 10 | ten | King | four |
| 9 | nine | Queen | plus or minus three |
| 8 | eight | Jack | two |
| 7 | seven | Ace | one |

A Queen dealt to the centre by the dealer as one of the two extra cards counts as plus three.

Players take up their hands and play commences with the 'eldest hand' (the player to the dealer's left) playing a card face up to the centre pile (if there are four players, of course, he begins the pile). He announces the combined total of the pile.

The object is to play cards to the centre pile to bring its total exactly to one of the several 'obstacles', which are 55, 66, 77, 88, 99 and 111. A player doing so scores a point, which is entered on the scoresheet. However if a player is forced to play a card which makes the total jump one of the obstacle numbers without landing on it, he loses a point and his score is adjusted accordingly.

Notice that a Queen can be used either to add three to the total or to subtract three, whichever the player wishes. He announces the new score as he plays the card. He scores a point for landing on the obstacle number or loses a point for jumping it, no matter whether he is going forwards or backwards (although it would be pointless for him to jump it backwards).

The deal ends when the score reaches or passes 111, and the cards are collected, shuffled and redealt by the next dealer, play restarting as before.

Some rules state that play does not terminate at 111, but continues with the score reverting to zero, but as with the cards remaining 55 is the only obstacle that can come into play, and even this depends on a low finishing total and no more than one Queen being used as a minus, it is better to terminate the hand at 111.

**Scoring** The winner is clearly the player with the most points. As a minus point is just about as likely as a plus point in this game, to prevent a mixture of plus and minus scores on the scoresheet, it is suggested that all players start with a score of plus 20, and go up and down from there. For the same reason it is better to decide that a game consists of a certain number of deals, say three for each player, rather than setting a points target for the winner.

# Old Maid

Old Maid is a game for children in which there is not a winner but a loser. The loser is the Old Maid, and is subject to derision – if it were a recently invented game, it would no doubt have a less politically incorrect title. It is not necessary for the penalty card to be a Queen, and in France it is a Jack.

| | |
|---|---|
| **Alternative names** | None |
| **Players** | Any number of three or more |
| **Minimum age** | Six years old |
| **Skill factor** | No skill needed |
| **Special requirements** | Two packs of cards if more than six players |

## Aim
To avoid being left at the end holding the odd Queen.

## Cards
The standard pack of 52 cards is used, from which is removed one Queen. If more than six play, it is better to use two packs of cards shuffled together, but again only one Queen is removed.

## Preparation
Anybody may pick up the cards, shuffle them and deal them one at a time face down to all the players until the pack is exhausted. It does not matter if some players get a card more than others.

## Play
The players look at their cards and discard face down on the table before them any pairs they may hold. If they hold three cards of the same rank they discard two of them and keep the third. Four of a kind are treated as two pairs.

The player to the dealer's left shuffles the cards remaining in his hand, and offers his hand as a fan face down to the player on his left. That player selects one card and adds it to his hand. If it matches a card he already holds, he pairs them together and discards them to the table. In any case, he then shuffles his hand and offers it face down as a fan to the player on his left, who selects a card, checks if it pairs with one of his, and if so discards them. He then offers his hand to the next player, and so on.

As play proceeds, and pairs are made, the players' hands will get progressively smaller, and players will drop out as all the cards in their hands are paired and discarded to the table. If a player holds only one card in his hand after pairing, the player on his left of course has no choice when it comes to receiving a passed-on card and the first player goes out of the game.

Eventually, all the cards will be paired except the odd Queen, and the player holding it is the loser, or 'old maid'.

Young children holding a Queen in their hand sometimes do not conceal their excitement when they manage to pass it on, and so the whereabouts of the Queen or Queens becomes the knowledge of all. This, if anything, usually adds to the general enjoyment.

# Omnibus Hearts

Hearts is best regarded as a family of games, since there are so many variations of it. Many of the variants have their own names, of which the best known is Black Maria. Already popular, it gained even more addicts when marketed with computer software. Omnibus Hearts, as its name suggests, incorporates features from many of the variants.

| | |
|---:|:---|
| **Alternative names** | Hit the Moon |
| **Players** | Three to six; four is best |
| **Minimum age** | Eleven years old |
| **Skill factor** | Skill is needed to play well |
| **Special requirements** | Pen and paper for scoring |

## Aim
To avoid taking tricks which contain penalty cards (♠Q and all the hearts) and to win the trick containing the bonus card (♦10).

## Cards
The standard pack of 52 cards is used, the cards ranking from Ace (high) to 2 (low). For four players the full 52 cards are used. For three players, the ♣2 is removed, to give hands of 17 cards each. For five players, both black 2s are removed, and hands are of ten cards each. For six players, ♣ 2, 3, ♦2, ♠2 are removed, and hands are of eight cards each (the ♥2 is retained as it is a penalty card).

## Preparation
Players draw cards from a spread pack to determine the first dealer. The drawer of the lowest card deals. The deal subsequently passes to the left.

The dealer shuffles and the player to his right cuts. The dealer then deals the whole pack clockwise, one at a time face down, to each player, beginning with the player to his left.

Players examine their cards and each passes on three cards face down to his right-hand neighbour. A player cannot pick up the cards passed to him until he himself has already passed on. With more than four players only two cards are passed.

## Play
The 'eldest hand' (the player to the dealer's left) leads to the first trick; see p155 for an explanation of tricks and trick-taking. There is no trump suit. Players must follow suit if able, and if unable may discard any card they wish. The trick is won by the highest card in the suit led, and the winner of a trick leads to the next.

The object is to avoid taking in a trick the ♠Q, which counts as −13 points to the player taking it, and any hearts, which count as −1 point each. On the other hand, to capture ♦10 is worth ten points.

A player who takes all fifteen counting cards (♠Q, ♦10 and all the hearts) scores 26 points instead of −16 as they would if counted normally. This is known as 'hitting the moon', 'take-all' or 'slam'.

The game ends when one player reaches a score of −100. The winner is the player with the smallest minus score (or, rarely, the highest plus score).

### Example hand
The hands are dealt as illustrated, using the Bridge convention of calling the players North, South, East and West.

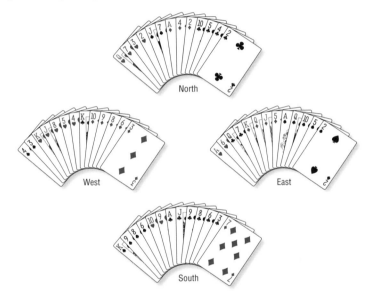

South is the dealer, and West the eldest hand. West would like diamonds to be led often so that he could win a trick with ♦10. He passes on the dangerous ♥K, J and ♣K. South keeps his clubs, as being relatively safe, and if he establishes them he might pick up ♦10. He passes ♥10, 9 and ♠K. East sees a chance of picking up ♦10 with his diamond court cards, and passes on ♠A, Q and ♥A. North has a hand which might not win a dangerous trick and passes on ♥Q, 7 and ♣10.

The hands are now as shown overleaf.

Omnibus Hearts

85

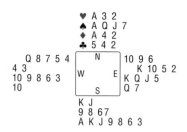

```
                    ♥ A 3 2
                    ♠ A Q J 7
                    ♦ A 4 2
                    ♣ 5 4 2
          Q 8 7 5 4      N        10 9 6
          4 3                     K 10 5 2
          10 9 8 6 3  W     E     K Q J 5
          10             S        Q 7
                    K J
                    9 8 6 7
                    A K J 9 8 6 3
```

West begins by leading his ♦9, and play proceeds:

| | West | North | East | South |
|---|---|---|---|---|
| 1 | ♦9 | ♦4 | ♦K | ♦7 |
| 2 | ♣10 | ♣5 | ♣Q | ♣J |
| 3 | ♥Q | ♣4 | ♣7 | ♣6 |

A slight shock for East who decides to exit with ♦5.

| | West | North | East | South |
|---|---|---|---|---|
| 4 | ♦3 | ♦2 | ♦5 | ♥K |

Another shock! East's best bet now seems to be to lead ♠5.

| | West | North | East | South |
|---|---|---|---|---|
| 5 | ♠4 | ♠J | ♠5 | ♠9 |
| 6 | ♥8 | ♣2 | ♠K | ♣A |

South now holds all the clubs. He leads ♠6.

| | West | North | East | South |
|---|---|---|---|---|
| 7 | ♠3 | ♠7 | ♠10 | ♠6 |
| 8 | ♥7 | ♠A | ♠2 | ♠8 |

With relief, North knows that his ♠Q is the only spade left, and he will not be caught with it, unless he is forced to lead it. He exits with ♥3.

| | West | North | East | South |
|---|---|---|---|---|
| 9 | ♥5 | ♥3 | ♥6 | ♥J |

South has only clubs left, and must make the rest of the tricks, which include both the ♦10 and the ♠Q.

The final scores are West 0, North −1, East −2 and South −13.

### Variants

Omnibus Hearts is itself a variant of Hearts, but players who wish to take in even more variants to the basic game might give minus values to the hearts suit of Ace −5, King −4, Queen −3, Jack −2 and the spot cards −1 each.

Some players prefer the ♦J or ♦8 to be the bonus card.

# Pelmanism

Pelmanism requires concentration and a good memory. It is popular with children, but should be played by those of similar ages, because older children will usually beat younger children, to the younger's frustration.

| | |
|---|---|
| **Alternative names** | Concentration, Memory, Pairs, Picking Pairs |
| **Players** | Two or more |
| **Minimum age** | Six years old |
| **Skill factor** | A good memory is needed |
| **Special requirements** | A playing surface large enough to lay out 52 cards |

## Aim
To collect as many pairs (two cards of the same rank) as possible.

## Cards
The standard pack of 52 cards is used.

## Preparation
The cards are shuffled by any player and laid out face down on the table. Some players prefer neat rows, but others think the game is improved if the cards are scattered haphazardly. The main requirement is that they do not touch each other.

## Play
One player begins the game by turning over any two cards, one at a time, so that all the other players can see them (there is no advantage to going first). If the two cards turned over are a pair, he removes them and puts them to one side to form his own individual pile. If not (and he must allow a moment or two for all players to note what ranks the cards are), he turns them face down again, without altering their position in the layout in any way.

If a player collects a pair, he has another turn and turns over two more cards. If he fails to collect a pair, the turn passes to the player on his left, who turns over two cards in the same way, adding any pairs to his own individual pile, and so on. When all the cards have been paired, and none remain on the table, the player with the highest number of pairs is the winner.

Good play consists of remembering the rank and position of all the cards previously turned over, so that when a player turns over a card of a rank equal to one which has been turned previously, he knows where that other card is, and can make a pair.

## Variants
For two or three players, a shorter game can be had by using a 40-card pack

(by removing the court cards) or a 32-card pack (by removing cards of ranks lower than 7). Older children, or adults, who think the game is rather simple and somewhat easy, can try turning up four cards at a time, and instead of collecting pairs can collect 'books', sets of all four cards of the same rank.

# Pig

Pig is a rather curious game which, according to a respected US card game rule book, is a simplification of an old game called Vive l'Amour ('Long Live Love'). Nevertheless, Pig is a children's game which is suitable for parties, and is not to be taken too seriously.

| | |
|---|---|
| **Alternative names** | Donkey |
| **Players** | Three to thirteen; four to seven is best |
| **Minimum age** | Seven years old |
| **Skill factor** | No skill needed |
| **Special requirements** | None |

## Aim
To collect four cards of the same rank, or to notice when another player does so.

## Cards
The standard pack of 52 cards is used, but is reduced to the number of cards equal to the number of players multiplied by four: four players use a 16-card pack, five players a 20-card pack and so on. This is achieved by removing as many ranks as necessary from the pack to make the total; for example, four players might strip everything but Aces and court cards from the pack, five players might strip everything except Aces up to 5s. Thirteen players would use the full pack.

## Preparation
Once the pack is of the required number of cards, any player may deal (there is no advantage to dealing, and the position of the players round the table is of no consequence). Four cards are dealt to each player, which exhausts the pack.

## Play
Players look at their cards. Simultaneously each then passes a card face down to his left for his left-hand opponent to take, at the same time taking into his hand the card passed to him by his right-hand opponent. This exchange must be synchronized, as no player must see the card he is receiving before he has passed his card on. Once this exchange has been made there is a brief pause for players to look at their cards and then it is repeated; the process continues to be repeated until one player has managed to acquire four cards of the same rank, called a 'book'.

Once a player manages this, he quietly and without any fuss stops exchanging and puts his finger to his nose. Other players, on noticing this, quietly do likewise. The last player to put his finger to his nose is the loser, and thus the Pig.

How this game arose from one called Vive l'Amour can only be imagined.

# Pip-Pip!

Pip-Pip! was invented or adapted from a European game before World War II, when it was described by Hubert Phillips, a prolific writer on card games, as 'one of the liveliest (and noisiest) of party games'. This disguises the fact that it is also a good and skilful game of the trick-taking type.

| | |
|---|---|
| **Alternative names** | None |
| **Players** | Any reasonable number; three to seven is best |
| **Minimum age** | Twelve years old |
| **Skill factor** | Some judgement needed |
| **Special requirements** | Pen and paper for scoring |

## Aim

To score points either by capturing tricks containing point-scoring cards or by changing the trump suit by holding and declaring the King and Queen of a suit other than the current trump suit.

## Cards

Two standard packs are required, shuffled together, making a joint pack of 104 cards. The cards rank in the order: 2 (high), Ace, King, Queen, Jack, 10, 9, 8, 7, 6, 5, 4, 3 (low).

## Preparation

From the shuffled pack, each player draws a card, the player who draws the highest being the first dealer: for this purpose cards rank as normal, Ace (high) to 2 (low). If there is a tie, a second draw is made between those who tied. Thereafter the deal passes to the left.

## Play

Before dealing the dealer shuffles the joint pack and offers it face down to the player to his left who cuts it, the top card of the lower half of the pack being turned over to denote trumps. The pack is reunited, the dealer reshuffles, the pack is cut by the player to his right, and the dealer deals seven cards face down one at a time to all players in a clockwise direction. The remaining cards are placed face down in the centre to form the stock.

The game is a trick-taking game, but in Pip-Pip! the cards rank in an unusual order, as the 2 is promoted from its usual place as lowest card to highest, as set out above.

There are two ways to score points. The first is to win tricks containing cards carrying a points value. These cards are:

| | |
|---|---|
| Deuces (2s) | eleven points each |
| Aces | ten points each |
| Kings | five points each |
| Queens | four points each |
| Jacks | three points each |

The 'eldest hand' (the player to the dealer's left) leads to the first trick by playing any card he wishes to the centre. The usual rules of trick-taking apply; see p155 for an explanation of tricks and trick-taking. Players must follow suit to the card led when able, and if unable, they may play a trump or discard. The trick is won by the highest trump it contains, or if there is none, by the highest card of the suit led.

If two identical cards (eg two ♠Ks) are played to the same trick, then the second card played is regarded as the higher.

The winner of the trick places the trick face down before him and draws the top card from stock, adding it to his hand. Each player in turn from his left then takes the top card of the stock into hand, thus maintaining all hands at seven cards. The winner of a trick leads to the next but before he does so he must pause as there is an opportunity to score points by a second method.

Any player who by virtue of the card he drew holds a King and Queen of the same suit (other than the trump suit) may lay them on the table before him and call 'Pip-Pip!'. By doing so he changes the trump suit to that of the suit of the cards he lays down. He also scores 50 points which are noted on the scoresheet.

Two or more players may call 'Pip-Pip!' at the same interval between tricks, in which case they all score 50 points. The trump suit changes to that of the last player to call, ie the player furthest to the left of the player who led.

A player who receives a matching King and Queen not of the trump suit in the initial deal may call 'Pip-Pip!' and change the trump suit (scoring 50 points as well) before the first trick is played.

When a player calls 'Pip-Pip!', the King and Queen remain face up on the table before him, but are still part of his hand, and he plays them to a trick whenever he wishes. The two cards can only be used once as a pair, and if he plays, say, the King and then draws the other King he cannot marry it up with the Queen on the table for a second 'Pip-Pip!' However he can 'Pip-Pip!' twice in the same suit, but only by playing both the second King and second Queen.

It is not compulsory for a player to declare 'Pip-Pip!' immediately he matches a King with a Queen. He may for tactical reasons hold back this declaration for a trick or two, but if he does so he risks being forced to play one or other of the cards and thus miss out on his 50 points.

Play continues in the manner described until the stock contains fewer cards than the number of players, making it impossible for each player to draw a card after a trick. The remaining few cards are then turned face up for all to see, but do not come into the game. The players play out their last seven cards without drawing.

**Scoring** When all the tricks have been played each player totals the number of points held in the tricks he won, and this total is added to his score. The total number of points to be won in this fashion is 264 (minus the values of any cards turned over at the end and not taken in tricks). There is a possible 400 to be made from 'Pip-Pips!', but not all will be made.

It is suggested that if a series of deals is required, then a game should continue until each player has dealt once.

**Example hand**

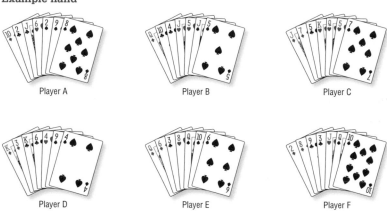

| Player A | Player B | Player C |
|----------|----------|----------|

| Player D | Player E | Player F |
|----------|----------|----------|

The cards are dealt to six players as in the illustration. The turn-up for trumps was a diamond. Player A is to lead first, but before he can do so Player C lays down his ♥K, Q and cries 'Pip-Pip!'. This immediately changes the trump suit to hearts and earns him 50 points on the scoresheet. Player A decides to lead his singleton ♦10 in the hope of being able to trump later. Play proceeds:

|   | *Player A* | *Player B* | *Player C* | *Player D* | *Player E* | *Player F* |
|---|------------|------------|------------|------------|------------|------------|
| 1 | ♦10 | ♦Q | ♦7 | ♦3 | ♦6 | <u>♦2</u> |

Players D and E might have attempted to win the trick with ♦K and ♦Q respectively but decided to hold them back with the prospect of gaining 50 points for a 'Pip-Pip!'. As it happens, they made the correct decision as Player F won with ♦2, and as he picked up ♦Q he assures himself of 15 points. The players draw cards from the stock as follows:

| Draw | ♥10 | ♦7 | ♠A | ♠K | ♣Q | ♥3 |
|------|-----|-----|-----|-----|-----|-----|

Player F decides to return the diamond suit when leading to trick 2:

|   |   |   |   |   |   |   |
|---|-----|-----|-----|-----|-----|-----|
| 2 | <u>♥6</u> | ♦7 | ♦J | ♦K | ♦Q | ♦8 |

A wonderful result for Player A, who trumped with ♥6 hoping that all the other players would have a diamond, and that maybe he would pick up some scoring cards. He did, picking up Jack, Queen, King and 12 points.

| Draw | ♠6 | ♠8 | ♣8 | ♠5 | ♠K | ♥2 |
|------|----|----|----|----|----|----|

Before Player A can lead to the next trick, Player E declares 'Pip-Pip!' placing his ♠K, Q before him. Spades are suddenly trumps, much to Player A's delight, since he holds four, including ♠2. He decides not to lead ♠2, rightly as it happens since he would not have picked up any other scoring cards with it. He decides to lead his singleton ♥10.

| 3 | ♥10 | ♥5 | ♥5 | ♥4 | ♥8 | ♥2 |
|---|-----|-----|-----|-----|-----|-----|

As last player, Player F decides to make his ♥2 for 11 points, and return his ♥3. Before he does so, however, he draws the top card from stock and is followed in turn by the other players.

The scores collected by each player in counting cards after three tricks are: Player A, 12 points, Player F 26 points, and the other players no points. However there have been two calls of 'Pip-Pip!, scoring 50 points each for Players C and E.

The game continues.

# Pontoon

Pontoon is probably a corruption of the French *Vingt-Un*, through the intermediate stage of Van John, which it was also called. It is likely that British soldiers of World War I picked up the name of the French version. This popular family gambling game often appears in British card books as Vingt-et-Un, although 99% of Britons actually know it as Pontoon. Blackjack is the much less interesting commercial version played in casinos, particularly in the USA. As with many games popular in pubs and houses, rules differ everywhere. Described here is a standard version.

| | |
|---:|:---|
| **Alternative names** | Blackjack, Twenty-One, Vingt-et-Un, Vingt-Un |
| **Players** | Three to ten; five or six is best |
| **Minimum age** | Ten years old |
| **Skill factor** | Some judgement needed |
| **Special requirements** | Cash, chips or counters for staking |

### Aim
To build a hand to beat the 'banker', which, apart from special hands, is a hand with a count nearer to, but not exceeding, 21.

### Cards
The standard pack of 52 cards is used. Cards have their pip values, with court cards counting as ten, and Aces as one or eleven at their holder's discretion.

### Preparation
Any player may pick up the cards, shuffle and begin to deal cards one at a time to each player round the table until a Jack appears. The player dealt the Jack becomes the first dealer, who is also the banker.

There is an advantage to holding the 'bank'. The bank passes from one player to another on the occurrence of a special hand called a 'pontoon', as will be explained below.

It is as well to agree a minimum and maximum initial stake which can be bet on a card.

### Play
The banker deals one card face down to each player, including himself. The players look at their cards but the banker does not. Each player announces a stake and places it before him. It should be between an agreed minimum and maximum. The banker then gives each player, and himself, a second face-down card. Again, the players look at their cards but the banker does not.

Players try to build a hand with a pip value of 21, or as near to it as possible without exceeding it. If a player holds a 'pontoon' (a two-card hand of 21, consisting of an Ace and a 10-count card) he declares it immediately and lays it on the table, usually with one card exposed. This is the highest hand and cannot be beaten, except by the banker also holding a pontoon.

The banker then deals with each player in turn, beginning with the player to his left.

A player who has been dealt a pair of Aces may 'split' them. He separates the cards and puts the same stake on the second card as on the first. The two cards now represent the first cards of two hands, so the banker deals a second card to each hand and deals with them separately. A player splitting Aces who receives another Ace to either hand can split further, and could (very rarely) hold four separate hands.

Each player has three choices when the banker comes to deal with him. He may:

| | |
|---|---|
| *Stand or stick* | This means he is happy with his count and 'stands' or 'sticks' with it, taking no more cards. He may not stand on a total lower then 16. |
| *Buy* | He may buy a further card face down, for a stake not exceeding his previous stake. He can buy further cards if he wishes, but always for a stake not exceeding his previous one. He may continue to buy until he has five cards, which is a special hand. A five-card hand, no matter what its total, beats all other hands except a pontoon. A player cannot buy a fifth card if his four-card total is 11 or lower. This is because he cannot lose, as he cannot exceed 21. He may, however, 'twist', which is to receive another card without buying it. |
| *Twist* | This is a request that the dealer twist the player a card face up, for which he does not pay. A player may twist at any time, whether or not he has previously bought a card, but he cannot buy a card after he has twisted. |

If while receiving cards a player's count exceeds 21, he has 'busted' and loses his stake. He passes his hand to the banker, who puts it face down on the bottom of the pack. He also passes over his stake.

When all the players have been dealt with (they do not show their hands), the banker turns over his two cards. If he has a pontoon, he immediately takes all the stakes of the players remaining in the game, including any players who also have a pontoon. Otherwise he may stand, or deal himself extra cards, standing when he wishes to. There is no restriction on when he may stand.

If the banker has a five-card hand, he loses to a pontoon but beats all other hands, including a player's five-card hand. Thus, should his count be 21, he will announce he is paying pontoons and five-card tricks only.

The banker wins on all ties.

Should the banker's count exceed 21, he busts and pays all players still in the game.

A player who holds a pontoon is paid double by the banker, except when the pontoon was part of a split hand. The banker is not paid double when he holds a pontoon, nor is a banker allowed to split Aces (he may still count them as 1 or 11).

The banker holds the bank until a player beats him with a pontoon, when that player may take over the bank if he wishes (he should, as it is usually profitable). Should two or more players hold a pontoon on the same deal, the player nearest to the banker's left has precedence.

The reason the bank is usually profitable, despite the fact that the players can choose their stakes according to their hands, is that the banker wins all tied hands, and wins from all players who bust, even though he might bust himself.

### Example hand

The illustration opposite shows how a deal with seven players might progress.

Player A stood on a two-card hand of 19.

Player B bought another card with a two-card total of 10, hoping for a 10-count card, but had to stand with 17.

Player C kept buying cards and was rewarded with a five-card hand.

Player D twisted (he is not allowed to stand) with the nasty count of 15, and bust.

Player E bought a second card with a count of 11 and was rewarded with a 10-count card for a total of 21.

Player F stood on a two-card hand of 18.

Player G split his Aces and eventually stood on both hands with disappointing counts of 16 and 20. He might have stood on the first, by counting his Ace as 11, with a total of 17, but twisted another card in the cope of a five-carder, only to get a 9 and settle with a count of 16, not risking busting in an attempt to get a five-carder.

The banker paid out on hands of 19 and over. So Player A won three units, Player B lost two, Player C won four, Player D lost three, Player E won two, Player F lost one, and Player G lost six on one hand, and won six on the other. The banker lost three units on the deal.

### Variants

i)  A common variant is to allow a third category of hand, a 'prial' of 7s, ie three 7s. This hand beats all. When held by a player the banker pays treble, but not vice-versa. Some regard this as unnecessary and feel it detracts from the best hand, pontoon, which after all is the name of the game.

ii) The banker looks at his first card when all players have staked on theirs, and may if he wishes demand all players double their stakes. This just gives him an additional advantage and is not recommended.

# Pontoon

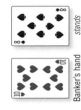

Banker's hand

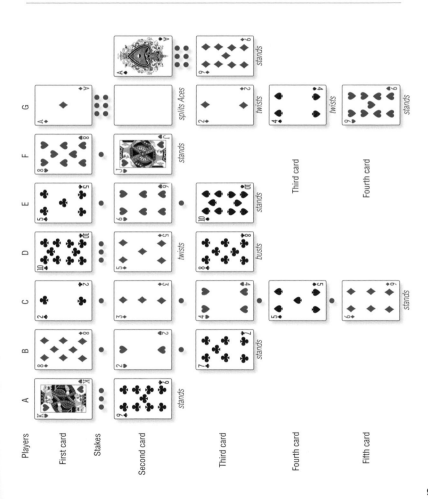

| Players | A | B | C | D | E | F | G | | |
|---|---|---|---|---|---|---|---|---|---|
| First card | K♦ | 8♦ | 2♣ | 10♣ | 5♣ | 8♥ | A♦ | A♠ | 9♦ |
| Stakes | | | | | | | | | |
| Second card | 9♣ | 2♥ | 3♦ | 5♦ | 6♥ | J♠ | | | *stands* |
| | *stands* | *stands* | | *twists* | | *stands* | *splits Aces* | | |
| Third card | | 7♣ | 4♥ | 8♣ | 10♠ | | 2♦ | | |
| | | *stands* | | *busts* | *stands* | | *twists* | | |
| Fourth card | | | 5♠ | | | | 4♣ | | |
| | | | | | | | *twists* | | |
| Fifth card | | | 6♦ | | | | 9♥ | | |
| | | | *stands* | | | | *stands* | | |

iii) An Ace and 10 is not regarded as a pontoon, which is limited to Ace and court card. Ace and 10 count as a normal 21.

iv) The banker is paid double when he holds a pontoon, except by a player holding a pontoon, who just loses his stake. This is not recommended for the same reason as ii) above.

v) Any pair may be split like Aces. This generally favours the banker, as it is not a good policy for the player to split cards other than Aces.

vi) The banker looks at his two-card hand before dealing with the players, and if he holds a pontoon exposes it and collects all stakes immediately. This is greatly in favour of the players, who avoid buying cards or splitting Aces in situations when they cannot win.

# President

President is a Western game based on the Chinese game of Zheng Zhangyou, and has been gaining in popularity since the 1970s. It is a game with very relaxed rules, and players tend to add or subtract rules as they wish. Its purpose is to rank the players in a hierarchy, and during the game players move up and down the social scale as they win or lose. These games have come to be called climbing games. During play there is always one at the top of the order, who sits in the best chair, and another at the bottom, who has to deal and do any other chore his betters may impose upon him. Players change position according to their status during the game.

| | |
|---|---|
| **Alternative names** | Arsehole, Bum, Scumbag and many similar others |
| **Players** | Four to seven |
| **Minimum age** | Twelve years old |
| **Skill factor** | Some skill needed |
| **Special requirements** | Ideally, an assortment of seating, so that President may have an armchair and Scumbag perhaps a beer crate, with grades in between; pen and paper for scoring |

### Aim
To be the first to reach eleven points; more immediately in each hand, to get rid of your cards as quickly as possible and thus become President, or at least to avoid being last and thus becoming Scumbag.

### Cards
The standard pack of 52 cards is used, the cards ranking 2 (high), A, K, Q, J, 10, 9, 8, 7, 6, 5, 4, 3 (low).

### Preparation
The first task is to determine the names for the ranks of the players. There must be one rank for each player. Since the game, under US influence, is often called President, President would suffice for the top rank, but it could be Monarch, Boss or whatever else the players prefer. Lower ranks could follow a company hierarchy, for example Vice President, Director, Manager, Foreman, Worker, Scumbag, or again whatever else might be preferred. The lowest rank usually carries a very demeaning name, of the Scum, Bum, Ratbag or Arsehole variety.

The player occupying the lowest position has to collect the cards after each hand, to shuffle and deal them for the next hand, and must perform any menial chores that might become necessary during the game. The seats should be arranged so that the best, most comfortable chair (reserved for the President) has the next most comfortable (say, the Vice President's) to its left, with each succeeding chair to the left being the standard lower than the previous one. Thus the worst chair (reserved for the Scumbag) is to the right of the President's chair.

For the first round of the game, players draw from a spread pack to determine their seats, with the highest (2 high, 3 low, as in the ranking above) taking the President's chair, and the others taking their seats in the order of the cards drawn, so the player drawing the lowest card will have the Scumbag's seat. Players who draw equal cards draw a second to determine precedence between them.

The player occupying the Scumbag's seat shuffles and deals the cards face down, one at a time clockwise, to all players until the whole pack is dealt. It does not matter that some players might receive a card more than other players. On subsequent deals it is always the player who is the Scumbag who deals.

### Play

The player to left of the dealer (ie he in the President's chair on the first round, the President himself thereafter) begins the play by leading any card, or set of cards of the same rank, face up to the table. Each player in turn to the left must then either play a card or cards to beat the previous card or pass. To beat a single card one must play a card of a higher rank. To beat a triple or four of a kind one must play a similar set of a higher rank. It is always necessary to play the same number of cards as was led. For example, if a pair of 5s is to be beaten, and a player holds three 8s, he can play two 8s and keep the third in hand, or he may pass. Passing is always allowed, and to pass does not prevent a player from playing on his next turn.

The play continues round the table as many times as necessary until a player lays a card or cards and every other player passes so the turn comes round to him again. All the cards played are then turned face down and put to one side and the player who played last begins a new round (for convenience often called a trick) by playing any card or matching cards to the table.

The first player to get rid of all his cards becomes President for the next deal. The next player becomes Vice President, and so on. If a player gets rid of his cards and all other players pass, of course that player cannot lead to a new trick as he has no more cards left. In this case, the first active player to his left leads to the new trick.

Play ends when all but one player have got rid of their cards and established their place in the hierarchy for the next deal. The player still with cards becomes the Scumbag. Players move to their new seats if necessary and the Scumbag shuffles and deals the next hands. When the deal is complete, the Scumbag then gives the President the highest card in his hand, and the President gives the Scumbag any card he likes in exchange. The President then leads to the first trick of the new deal.

**Scoring** A system of scoring over a number of deals is to award the President two points on every deal and the Vice President one point. Others score nothing. The first to eleven points is the overall winner.

**Strategy** It is important to get rid of low cards as quickly as possible. A player with a 3 can only play it by getting the lead, and to get the lead a player must play a card or set of cards which the others players cannot beat. Therefore cards which are likely to win the lead, such as a pair of 2s or Aces, should be played with this purpose.

**Example hand**
Four hands are dealt as shown, using the Bridge convention of calling the players North, South, East and West.

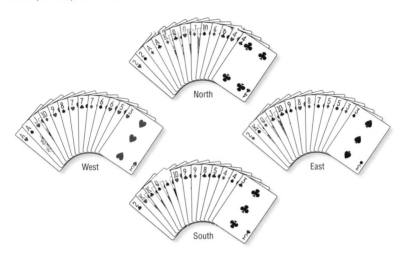

North is the President, and therefore is to lead. Play proceeds, with the underlining indicating the end of a trick, ie when three players have passed consecutively. The player who last played leads to a new trick.

| North | East | South | West |
|---|---|---|---|
| 4–4 | 5–5 | 9–9 | Pass |
| Q–Q | Pass | Pass | <u>Pass</u> |
| 6–6 | 8–8 | Pass | Pass |
| <u>Pass</u> | 3–3 | 4–4 | 6–6 |
| A–A | Pass | Pass | <u>Pass</u> |
| 10 | J | Q | Pass |
| K | 2 | Pass | Pass |
| <u>Pass</u> | 7 | 8 | 9 |
| J | Q | 2 | Pass |
| Pass | <u>Pass</u> | 3 | 5 |
| 2 | Pass | Pass | <u>Pass</u> |
| 2 (out) | Pass | Pass | <u>Pass</u> |
| | 9 | 10 | J |

| North | East | South | West |
|-------|------|-------|------|
| | K | Pass | A |
| | Pass | Pass | 3 |
| | 10 (out) | J | A |
| | | Pass | 7–7–7 |
| | | Pass | 8 |
| | | K | Pass |
| | | K | Pass |
| | | 5 (out) | |

So North is President, East is Vice President, South is Worker and West is Scumbag. North retains the comfy chair as President, while West as Scumbag must collect the cards, shuffle and deal the next hand. North has two points towards overall victory and East one point.

In the example hand, West held up his pair of Aces because it was more or less his only chance of getting the lead. Had he played them earlier, and been beaten by North's pair of 2s, he might never have got the lead at all and was certain to become the Scumbag. Timing is all.

**Variants**

President is a game which lends itself to idiosyncratic rules and variations. Some of the more commonly found are listed:

*Jokers*  Some players include one or two Jokers in the pack. When included, Jokers rank above the 2s. If Jokers are used, the Scumbag, if dealt one, need not hand it over to the President, but must hand over his next highest card. Some players prefer the Jokers to be wild cards, thus 9–9–Joker can be played as three 9s.

*Sequences*  Another combination which can be played is a sequence of three or more cards. In this case a four-card sequence of, say, J–10–9–8, can only be beaten by a four-card sequence of higher rank such as K–Q–J–10. A four-card sequence doesn't beat a three-card sequence. The number of cards in the sequence cannot change during the course of the trick. If sequences are allowed, sometimes multiple sequences are as well, for example two or more sequences of equal length and rank, such as 3–4–5, 3–4–5, or put another way, 33–44–55. This particular multiple sequence can be beaten only by another pair of identical sequences of a higher rank, for example 7–8–9, 7–8–9. Sequences are a regular feature of the Chinese game Zheng Zhangyou.

*Opening lead*  Rather than the President always leading to the first 'trick', the player who holds the ♣3 makes the initial lead, either with a single card or a combination including ♣3.

*Single round play*  Some players prefer that after a lead, players get one opportunity to beat the lead. Once the play reaches the leader, he does not get a second chance to play to the trick, which ends. The last player to play to the trick leads to the next one. Some players stay with the multi-round play as described, but do not allow a player who passes to play at a subsequent turn in the same trick. Others prefer a rule which states that a player cannot pass if he can beat the previous play.

*Equal play*    Some players allow a card or a combination to 'beat' a card or combination of equal rank. By this means a player can play 5–5, for example, on a previous 5–5.

*Card*          Some players prefer that after the deal the Scumbag must
*exchange*      give the President his two best cards, rather than one, and the second-to-last player must give the Vice President his best card in exchange for whatever the Vice President wishes to give him.

*Scoring*       Some players give the winner of a hand three points, the second two and the third one. In this case, a target for game might be 21.

# Rams

Rams is similar to a gambling game called Loo, which dates back to the 17th century and is still played. Popular in central Europe as a drinking game, Rams is one of the many trick-taking games in which a hand consists of five cards.

| | |
|---|---|
| **Alternative names** | Rammes, Ramsch, Reins, Rounce |
| **Players** | Three to five |
| **Minimum age** | Twelve years old |
| **Skill factor** | Some skill needed |
| **Special requirements** | Sufficient counters (or matchsticks) to give each player 25 |

## Aim
To win counters from other players by winning tricks.

## Cards
A shortened pack of 32 cards is used, formed by removing the ranks from 2 to 6 from a standard pack. The cards rank from Ace (high) to 7 (low).

## Preparation
Each player is given 25 counters to begin the game. Any player may take the cards, shuffle, and deal them round face up clockwise to each player until a Jack appears. The player to whom it is dealt becomes the first dealer. Thereafter the deal passes clockwise.

## Play
The dealer places five counters into the centre to form a pool. The dealer shuffles, the player to his right cuts and, beginning with the 'eldest hand' (the player on his left), the dealer deals five cards face down to each player clockwise and finally to a 'widow' (an extra hand) in batches of three cards then two.

The remaining cards are placed to one side face down, and are not used. The top card of the pile, however, is turned face up to denote the trump suit.

Players examine their hands and, beginning with the eldest hand, must decide whether to play the hand or pass. To play is to undertake to win at least one trick. A player who does not wish to play places his hand face down in front of him.

Any player on his turn may exchange his hand for the widow (he is not allowed to look at the widow first). If a player takes the widow, he may not pass and is obliged to play. If everybody passes up to the player on the dealer's right, then that player must play, otherwise he must pay the dealer five counters to pass (he might as well play, because it would only cost him five counters if he played and failed to win a trick).

If only one player has decided to play when it is the dealer's turn to decide, then the dealer must play. In this case he has the privilege of taking the card denoting the trump suit into his hand, discarding an unwanted card in its place.

There is one other option open to each player on his turn during this round of stating whether he plays or not. A player may declare 'rams'. This is an undertaking to win all five tricks. When a player declares 'rams', all players must play. Any players who have previously passed must take up their hands again and play.

When it is settled as to who is playing and who isn't, the trick-taking phase begins. If a player has declared 'rams', he leads to the first trick. Otherwise the active player nearest to the dealer's left leads to the first trick.

The usual rules of trick-taking do not apply to Rams; see p155 for an explanation of tricks and trick-taking. In Rams, each player must follow suit if possible, and moreover must play a card higher than that currently heading the trick, if possible. If he can follow suit, but the suit led has already been trumped, he is not obliged to beat the highest card led in the suit. If he cannot follow suit, and a trump has already been played he must play a higher trump, if possible. If he cannot follow suit and has a trump but not one to beat the highest trump already played, he must still play a losing trump. Only if a player cannot follow suit or trump is he allowed to discard.

A trick is won by the player who contributed the highest trump to it, or if no trumps were played, the highest card in the suit led.

**Scoring** The amount in the pool may vary, but will always be divisible by five. At the end of each deal, each player takes one fifth of the pool for each trick he won. Then any player who played (as opposed to passing) and failed to win a trick must put five counters into the pool for the next hand (to which will be added the five the next dealer puts in – this is how the amount in the pool varies). Players who passed do not have to contribute to the pool.

In the case of a player declaring 'rams', if he wins he takes the whole pool plus five counters from each of the other players; if he loses a trick, play of that hand ends and he must add to the pool the same number of counters as were already there, and give each other player five counters.

Play may continue for an agreed number of deals (say four each for three players, three each for four, two each for five), when the winner is the player with the most counters.

If a player loses all his counters, there could be a second issue of an equal amount of counters to all players to allow the player who lost his counters to continue for the required number of deals.

Rams

### Example hand

Four hands are dealt as illustrated, using the Bridge convention of calling them North, East, South and West. The trump suit is hearts.

North

West

East

South

West is first to call and thinks hard about whether or not to call 'rams'. If the trump suit had been diamonds or clubs he might have risked it, but as the odds are heavily against another player not having two trumps he wisely decides against it and merely decides to play. With two Kings and the trump Queen, North also decides to play. East is hopeful his ♠A will win or that he will be able to trump an early club lead and decides to play, although it is a big risk (in fact, strictly speaking he should pass, as he is unlikely to win more than one counter and stands to lose five, and the odds of him winning a trick must be less than 5 to 1 on). South, who was the dealer, passes, as he has little chance of making a trick. The play goes as follows:

|   | West | North | East |
|---|------|-------|------|
| 1 | ♦A | ♦K | ♦8 |
| 2 | ♣A | ♣9 | ♥10 |
| 3 | ♥K | ♠10 | ♠A |
| 4 | ♦J | ♥Q | ♦10 |
| 5 | ♣J | ♣K | ♠8 |

So West and North each take two counters from the pool and East one, as he managed to take a club by trumping it.

106

It is interesting to note that had West declared 'rams' and led his ♥K, followed by ♦A, J, and then ♣A he would win the first four tricks. Whether or not he would have succeeded in getting all five tricks would depend upon which card North discarded on the ♦J. He held ♣K, 9 and ♠10. Had he discarded ♣9 West would have succeeded. But an experienced player would know that West would not call 'rams' holding a bare spade lower than 10, and would have discarded ♠10 and so defeated West's attempt to take all five tricks.

# Ranter Go Round

Ranter Go Round is a children's game said to have been invented in Cornwall, where it is also called Cuckoo. However, Cuckoo is a game which is played in many countries in Europe, sometimes with special cards, such as the Italian *Cuccu* pack, which dates from the 17th century.

| | |
|---|---|
| **Alternative names** | Chase the Ace, Cuckoo |
| **Players** | Any reasonable number; five to twenty is best |
| **Minimum age** | Seven years old |
| **Skill factor** | No skill needed |
| **Special requirements** | Counters; a bowl or saucer |

## Aim
To be the last player left in, by not holding the lowest card when the cards are revealed at the end of each deal.

## Cards
The standard pack of 52 cards is used, the cards ranking from King (high) to Ace (low).

## Preparation
A saucer or similar should be placed in the centre of the table. Each player is given three counters, which represent three 'lives'.

Any player may become the first dealer by agreement, but if there is a dispute any player may pick up the cards, shuffle and begin to deal cards one at a time to each player round the table until a Jack appears. The player dealt the Jack becomes the first dealer. The deal subsequently passes to the left.

The dealer shuffles the cards. Each player is then dealt one card, face down. The remainder of the cards are put into a pile to one side.

## Play
Each player looks at his card. Play begins with the 'eldest hand' (the player to the dealer's left), who has the choice of keeping his card (which he will do if he considers it unlikely to be the lowest dealt) or of exchanging it with the card of the player to his left. This he does by offering it face down to him and saying 'change'. The player asked to change must do so unless he holds a King, when he can reply 'King', forcing the player who wished to change to keep his card.

Each player in turn has the opportunity to keep his card or pass it on. Obviously, a player who has to pass on a card to the preceding player and who receives a higher card than that he passed on in exchange will not wish to pass on his new card on his go, as he knows it is not the lowest.

A player who is asked to change and who returns to the player on his right an Ace, 2 or 3 must announce the rank of the card passed on. Each succeeding player then knows whether or not his own card is safe, and on his own turn will ask to change only if the card he holds is equal to or lower than the card whose value was announced.

The dealer is the last to play, and if he wishes to exchange his card he must do so by cutting the part of the pack not dealt and taking the top card of the lower part of the pack. He must show the card he draws, and if it is a King he is the loser and puts one of his counters into the saucer. Otherwise, all players show their cards and the player with the lowest loses a 'life' and puts a counter into the saucer. If there are equal lowest, they all put in a counter.

The deal passes clockwise, and a player who loses his three counters must drop out of the game. The winner is the last person left in. Children generally do not mind dropping out, as a new game comes round quite quickly.

# Rockaway

Rockaway is a children's version of the various games of the Switch family.

| | |
|---|---|
| **Alternative names** | Crazy Aces, Go Boom |
| **Players** | Two to eight; four to six is best |
| **Minimum age** | Eight years old |
| **Skill factor** | Little skill needed |
| **Special requirements** | Pen and paper for scoring |

### Aim
To get rid of all the cards in your hand.

### Cards
The standard pack of 52 cards is used, the cards ranking from Ace (high) to 2 (low). If five or more play, then two packs shuffled together can be used.

### Preparation
Any player may pick up the cards, shuffle and begin to deal cards one at a time to each player round the table until a Jack appears. The player dealt the Jack becomes the first dealer. If a series of deals is played, and a running score kept, the deal subsequently passes to the left.

The dealer deals the cards clockwise, face down, one at a time to each player beginning with the 'eldest hand' (the player to the dealer's left) until each player, including himself, has seven cards. He then turns over the next card, which is called the 'widow', and places it face up in the centre of the table. The remaining cards are placed face down beside it to form the 'stock'.

### Play
The eldest hand begins play by placing on the widow a card of the same suit or rank as the widow, or an Ace. If he cannot, he must draw a card from the top of the stock, and must continue to draw cards from the stock until he draws one which allows him to cover the widow. The next player to the left must then play a card of the same suit or rank as the new card at the top of the widow, or an Ace, and if he is unable to he must draw until he can, and so on.

When the stock is exhausted, a player unable to lay a legitimate card on the widow at his turn merely passes. If the game becomes blocked, and nobody can go, the player who last played a card to the widow lays any card he wishes, and the game proceeds as usual.

The first player to get rid of all his cards is the winner.

**Scoring** If a series of deals is required, the game can last until each player has dealt once. At the end of each hand a running score is kept for each player, with each player debited with a score against them according to the cards they hold. Each Ace counts 15, court cards ten, and other cards their pip value. When all players have dealt, the player with the lowest minus score is the winner.

**Strategy** A player should try to keep in his hand cards in as many suits and rank as possible, to ensure that he has the maximum chance of being able to play a card on his turn. If he holds a card in each suit he is certain to be able to play a card on his next turn.

**Example hand**

Suppose hands are dealt to five players, as shown.

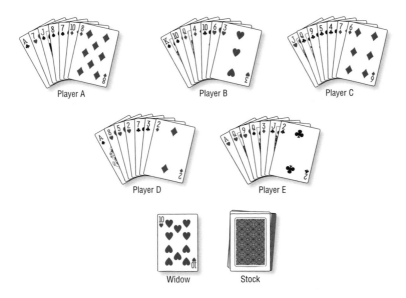

| Player A | Player B | Player C |

| Player D | Player E |

| Widow | Stock |

The ♥10 is the widow, and Player A is to play first. The play might proceed:

| | Player A | Player B | Player C | Player D | Player E |
|---|---|---|---|---|---|
| 1 | ♥7 | ♥6 | ♦6 | ♦2 | ♣2 |
| 2 | ♣A | ♣10 | ♣Q | ♣7 | ♣J |
| 3 | ♠J | ♠10 | | | |

Player C becomes the first player who cannot play and must draw cards from the top of the stock until he can, when play will proceed.

It was good play of Player E to play his ♣2 on the ♦2 on the first round, as this meant he kept a card of each suit in his hand. Had he played ♦3 instead, he would have been 'void' (without a card) in diamonds. Player A should perhaps have played his ♦10 to lead, as playing ♥7 left him void in hearts.

It was also good play, though less obvious, of Player B to play ♠10 rather than ♠K on his third round. This is because he had already played one 10, and another was the widow, leaving only one more to come. As there are three Kings to come, it is more likely that he will be able to play a King rather than a 10 in future play.

Obviously, Aces are valuable because they can be played on any card, and so should not be played if there is another option. In the example hand, Player A had no alternative to playing his ♣A on the second round.

### Variants
**Go Boom** Go Boom is the US name for Rockaway, but is also the name by which this variant of the basic game is known. It is played slightly differently. It is limited to six players, and is a good game for introducing children to the principles of trick-taking. There is no widow and the Ace has no special properties.

The eldest hand has the first lead and all players must play a card of the same suit or rank as the card led (not of the previous card played). If unable to play such a card, a player draws cards from the stock until he can go, as in the basic game.

When all players have played to the card led, the cards form a trick, and are collected up. The trick itself is worthless and put to one side, but the player who 'won' it, ie who played the highest card of the suit led, has the advantage of leading to the next, and can lead whichever card he likes.

As in the basic game, when the stock is exhausted a player who cannot go misses his turn. The player who gets rid of all his cards first is said to 'go boom' and is the winner. Unlike Rockaway, the game cannot be blocked, as each trick is separate and there is always a winner to lead to the next.

A series of games can be played with players debited with points at the end of each deal as described above, and a running score kept.

# Rolling Stone

Rolling Stone is unrelated to the pop group, though it has the similar quality of being something that goes on nearly forever... Its alternative names are French and German words which mean 'swollen' or 'to swell', and the game's characteristic is that as soon as a player thinks he is about to get rid of his cards and win the game, his hand suddenly swells in number and he is back where he started.

| | |
|---|---|
| **Alternative names** | Énflé, Schwellen |
| **Players** | Four to six |
| **Minimum age** | Ten years old |
| **Skill factor** | A good memory is needed to play well |
| **Special requirements** | None |

## Aim
To get rid of all your cards by playing them to the table.

## Cards
The standard pack of 52 cards is used, from which cards are removed depending on the number of players; each player must have eight cards. For four players, therefore, the 6s, 5s, 4s, 3s and 2s are removed, leaving a pack of 32 cards. For five players, the 4s, 3s and 2s are removed, leaving a pack of 40 cards. For six players, the 2s are removed, leaving a pack of 48 cards.

The cards rank from Ace (high) down to the 7s, 5s or 3s (low) according to the size of the pack.

## Preparation
The cards are shuffled and each player draws a card from the spread pack; the player who draws the highest becomes the dealer.

The dealer deals the cards one at a time, face down, in a clockwise direction to all players until the pack is exhausted. Each player will have eight cards.

## Play
The 'eldest hand' (the player to the dealer's left) leads to the first 'trick', although it is not a trick in the usual sense as we shall see; see p155 for an explanation of tricks and trick-taking. All other players must follow suit if they can. If all follow suit, the player who played the highest card 'wins' the trick. He collects up the cards and puts them to one side face down. They play no further part in the game. The trick itself is of no value, but it allows the winner to lead to the next trick.

If a player cannot follow suit to the card led, he must pick up all the cards that have been played to the trick and add them to his hand. He then leads to the next trick by playing any card he likes, except a card of the suit he has just picked up.

Play continues until one player has got rid of all his cards, and is the winner.

A deal is almost always a game in itself (ie cumulative scores aren't kept over a series of deals) because with good players a deal can last a long time. By watching which suits other players have to pick up, all players can get a reasonable idea of the suits other players hold. A player down to one card will almost certainly not find his suit led and will be forced to pick up cards of another suit; he must then lead what was his singleton card, since he is not allowed to lead the suit he picked up, so all other players then know exactly what cards he holds. When each player's cards are more or less known by all the others the game could be everlasting...

**Variants**
The game is often played for stakes, with each player placing a chip into a pool which is taken by the winner. Alternatively, the winner can collect a chip for every card each loser holds in his hand at the finish. Some players allow a player picking up the incomplete trick to lead the same suit to the following trick.

# Romanian Whist

Players who like Nomination Whist might like to try Romanian Whist, which follows similar principles, but has a different scoring system.

| | |
|---|---|
| **Alternative names** | None |
| **Players** | Three to six |
| **Minimum age** | Eleven years old |
| **Skill factor** | Good judgement needed |
| **Special requirements** | Two pens (of different colours) and paper for scoring |

## Aim
To score points by forecasting correctly the number of tricks you will make on each deal.

## Cards
From a standard pack are stripped sufficient cards of the lowest ranks to leave a pack of eight times as many cards as there are players. For example, for three players 24 cards are needed, so the 2s, 3s, 4s, 5s, 6s, 7s and 8s are removed, leaving just the Aces, Kings, Queens, Jacks, 10s and 9s. For six players 48 cards are needed, so the 2s only need be stripped. The cards rank A (high), K, Q, J, 10, 9.... down to the lowest rank required for the number of players.

## Preparation
Any player may pick up the shortened pack and deal the cards round face up one at a time among the players until a Jack appears. The player who receives the Jack becomes the first dealer and thereafter the deal passes clockwise.

## Play
The dealer deals the cards face down to each player. The number of cards varies. The first few deals (the number of deals corresponding to the number of players) are of one card each, eg if there are three players, the first three deals are of one card each. Thereafter the number of cards dealt increases by one until it reaches a maximum of eight, whereupon it diminishes by one until it reaches one again. The number of deals of one card at the end is again equal to the number of players. Thus, if there are three players, the game consists of 19 deals, with the number of cards dealt on each round being 1, 1, 1, 2, 3, 4, 5, 6, 7, 8, 7, 6, 5, 4, 3, 2, 1, 1, 1.

After each deal, the unused cards are placed face down in the centre, and the dealer turns over the top card to indicate the trump suit for that deal. If all the cards are dealt, as will be the case when the deal consists of eight cards each, the hand is played with no trumps.

Romanian Whist is a trick-taking game, in which the normal rules of trick-taking apply; see p155 for an explanation of tricks and trick-taking. The 'eldest hand' (the player to the dealer's left) leads to the first trick by playing any card he wishes to the table. The following players in clockwise order complete the trick by adding a card to it; if possible they must follow suit, if they cannot they may play a trump or discard as they please. Each trick is won by the highest trump it contains, or if it does not contain a trump by the highest card of the suit led. The winner of a trick collects the cards, places them face down before him and leads to the next trick.

After each deal, and before the trick-taking phase begins, each player in turn, beginning with the eldest hand, must state exactly how many tricks he 'contracts' to make on that deal (note: he does not state a minimum, he states an exact number). The numbers are noted on the scoresheet. The dealer, who bids last, may not bid a number that brings the total number of tricks contracted for up to the number of cards dealt. This prevents a situation in which everybody could make the number of tricks they contracted for.

**Scoring** When the trick-taking stage is complete, each player who correctly forecast exactly the number of tricks he would make, scores five points plus one for each trick made. A player whose forecast is wrong loses points equivalent to the number he bid, plus, if he made more tricks then he forecast, one point for each 'overtrick'. The player who ends with most points is the winner.

Two pens of different colours are recommended for scoring. The bids made by each player can then be entered in one colour and their actual score in the other.

There is no restriction on the number of times a player may bid zero (which most players regard as the easiest number to make). The reason for the several rounds where only one card is dealt is to ensure that each player has to deal one card an equal number of times. This evens out the frustration of the dealer who often is forced by the rules to bid 'one' when he has practically no prospect of making a trick.

### Example hand
In a game with four players the round has been reached where each player has six cards. The cards are dealt as in the illustration opposite, using the Bridge convention of calling the players North, East, South and West. South dealt, and the trump suit is clubs.

West has a certain trick with the ♣A, a pretty sure one with ♥A, but has four awkward middling cards in diamonds and spades (remember 7 is the smallest rank dealt). He has a difficult choice and calls 'three'. North might make a trump trick if diamonds are led and could make another with ♠A or K, but as West has already called three, he contents himself with a bid of 'one'. East, on a spade lead could make a trump trick, but is confident his sevens will prevent him making a trick in the red suits, especially with four tricks being bid already, and he calls 'one'. South is not allowed to call 'one', as that would bring the total of tricks bid to six, the number of cards dealt to each. 'One' would have been his choice, as he should make a trick in diamonds if they are led and could make one with his ♣Q if spades are led. On the other hand if West leads ♣A on the first trick, as is possible on his bid of three, he could make nothing. On the grounds that he holds half the diamonds in the pack, and that they might be trumped, he decides to call 'nil'. Five tricks are bid so at least one player will make more than he wants.

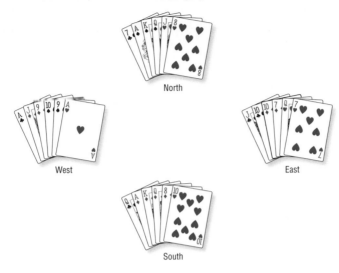

North

West

East

South

The play proceeds as follows:

| | West | North | East | South |
|---|---|---|---|---|
| 1 | ♥A | ♥J | ♥Q | ♥10 |
| 2 | ♠9 | ♠A | ♣J | ♦A |
| 3 | ♣A | ♣7 | ♣10 | ♣Q |
| 4 | ♠10 | ♠K | ♦10 | ♦K |
| 5 | ♦9 | ♥8 | ♥7 | ♦Q |

North did not expect to make ♥8, and has now made a trick more than he bargained for. Worse is to come.

| 6 | ♦J | ♠Q | ♦7 | ♦8 |
|---|---|---|---|---|

So West called 'three' and made two. North called 'one' and made three. East called 'one' and made one. South called 'nil' and made nil. It was a very unusual hand resulting in the scores: East six; South five; West minus three and North minus three.

# Rummy

Rummy is the family name of that popular group of games in which players take cards from a stock or a discard pile and try to meld them in sets or sequences. Yet the name was unknown before 1900. The game is descended from a game called Coon Can and spread rapidly in South and North America where it acquired the name Rum, probably from the alcoholic drink. It is one of the best-known and most-played of all card games, and there are countless variants. What might be called the basic game is described first.

| | |
|---|---|
| **Alternative names** | Rum |
| **Players** | Two to six |
| **Minimum age** | Ten years old |
| **Skill factor** | A skilful game |
| **Special requirements** | Pen and paper for scoring |

## Aim
To play all your cards to the table by melding them into groups and sequences.

## Cards
The standard pack of 52 cards is used, the cards ranking from King (high) to Ace (low).

## Preparation
Each player draws a card from a spread pack; the player who draws the lowest card becomes the first dealer. The deal subsequently passes to the left.

The dealer shuffles and the player to his right cuts. The dealer deals one card at a time clockwise, face down, until each has the following number of cards: with two players, ten each; with three or four players, seven each; with five or six players, six cards each.

The dealer places the remainder of the pack face down in the centre to form the 'stock'. The top card of the stock is turned over and placed beside it to become the first card of a discard pile.

## Play
Each player in turn, beginning with the 'eldest hand' (the player to the dealer's left) and proceeding clockwise, has the opportunity to take into his hand the top card of the discard pile, or if he doesn't want it, the top card from the stock. He then discards a card from his hand to the discard pile, which becomes available to the next player to play.

On his turn, between drawing a card and discarding, a player may 'meld', which is to lay down before him on the table sets of cards, which can be groups of three or four cards of the same rank, or sequences of three or more cards of the same suit (Ace being low). These sets are called melds. In this interval between drawing and discarding, a player may also add a card or cards to any melds he has on the table, or 'lay off' cards onto melds of other players. He can do any or all of these things on the same turn. When a player goes out, the hand ends and opponents cannot lay off cards onto his (or other players') melds.

The first player to get rid of all his cards, called 'going out', wins the hand. On his last turn he can discard as normal but is not obliged to   he may meld all the cards in his hand.

Should the stock become exhausted before any player has managed to go out, the player who took the last card turns over the discard pile which becomes the stock, and his discard begins a new discard pile. Play then proceeds as normal.

**Scoring** When a player goes out, other players are debited with the cards held in their hands. For this purpose court cards count as ten points and all other cards with their pip value (Ace counting one). If a running score is kept, the winner is the player with the lowest debit score when another player passes 100. If the game is played for stakes, it is usual for the losers to pay the winner after each hand.

**Strategy** A player's task is to assess which cards in his hand give him the best chance of melding, and he should try to build his hand to improve those chances.

Hand                    Discard pile        Stock

The holder of the hand in the illustration should certainly take the ♥4 from the discard pile and discard ♠K. The ♥4 doubles the player's chances of melding, as ♥3 or ♥6 will provide a sequence, whereas only one card, ♠Q, will complete the sequence with ♠K and ♠J. Moreover the exchange reduces the count of the hand by six points should an opponent go out. The ♠J should be discarded at the earliest opportunity afterwards.

Players should note which cards have already been discarded. For example, in the hand illustrated, if the ♥3 and ♥6 have already been discarded or taken from the discard pile by another player, it would be pointless to take the ♥4. It would be better to take the top card of the stock. However, two cards counting ten points each, such as ♠K, J, with only one card available to meld with them, should not be held for more than a round or two.

On the other hand, a collection of court cards providing an opportunity to meld should not be broken up too quickly just for the sake of reducing the adverse point count. Suppose a player holds the hand illustrated overleaf, for example, and draws from the stock ♥J. Adding ♥J to the two Queens and ♦10 that he holds increases the number of cards which would allow him to meld from these cards to five from the current three. To retain the ♥J and discard the ♠7, which is useless to him, would be a sound move, despite increasing his liabilities if another player goes out. Of course, the state of the game and the proximity to going out of another player will also affect the decision. In particular, if the player suspects his left-hand opponent is able to use the ♠7 he might decide not to discard it. In this case, his best discard would be ♦10, which needs one specific card, the ♦J, to be drawn to be of any use. In any case, to reject the card drawn, the ♥J, as many players might without thinking, would be a mistake.

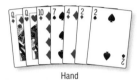

Hand                    Draw

Two cards in sequence need the addition of one of two cards to make a meld (unless they include the King or Ace), as do two cards of the same rank. But the two in sequence is better to hold since, if a card is acquired to make a meld of three, there still remain two more cards which will increase the meld to four, whereas a meld of a group of three cards of equal rank leaves only one other card which will improve it to a group of four.

Melds do not have to be played to the table as soon as they are acquired and sometimes if a player holds a combination of cards which can be melded in different ways it might pay to keep the melds in hand for a round or two to see what other cards might be obtained. Holding melds in hand also prevents opponents laying off to them. However, melds in hand become debits if another player surprisingly goes out, so delaying declaring them is taking a chance.

### Variants

There are many variants of Rummy. Some have their own names, and are described below. Other common variations to the basic game described above include:

*Laying off*    Laying off on opponents' melds is not permitted, except when a player goes out. In that case other players can lay off cards to the winner's melds only.

*Going out*    A player must make a discard on going out. This means that a player holding two cards cannot go out except by laying off.

*Deadwood*    Players do not 'declare' their melds but keep them in their hands. When a player goes out, the other players then lay down their melds, lay off if possible on the winner's melds, and are debited with the unmelded cards remaining in their hands, called 'deadwood'.

*Going rummy*  A player who melds all his cards and goes out in one turn, without having previously melded, is said to have 'gone rummy', and his opponents' debits are doubled.

*Stock*  Play ends if the stock is exhausted. The winner is the player with *exhaustion*  the lowest count of unmelded cards.

**Knock Rummy**  Knock Rummy, also known as Poker Rum, is best for three to five players. Each receives seven cards. Players do not meld during the game. A player goes out by 'knocking', ie he knocks on the table after making his draw. He then lays down his melds and may discard.

The main difference from the basic game is that the player going out is allowed to have an unmatched card or cards, with which he is debited. It is possible for the player, picking up a hand of all low-count cards, to knock immediately, even without a meld at all.

When a player knocks, other players lay down their melds and are debited with their deadwood (unmatched cards). There is no laying off. If the game is for stakes, players pay the winner according to the differences in their scores (if a cumulative score is being kept, the losers are debited with the difference).

It is possible that the knocker will not have the lowest count. If so, the player with the lowest count is the winner, and the others settle accordingly, with the knocker paying an additional ten units (or, if scoring, being debited with an additional ten points). If the knocker and another player tie, the other player is the winner, but the knocker does not have to pay the ten points penalty. If two or more players other than the knocker tie, they share the winnings if playing for stakes.

If a player knocks and 'goes rum' (ie does not have any unmatched cards) the other players pay him a bonus of 25 units (or 25 points) in addition to the difference in their counts. A 'rum hand' cannot be tied, so if another player also has a hand with no unmatched cards, he must pay the knocker the 25-point bonus too (apart from an accident, this could also happen because the unfortunate player so caught has not yet had a turn).

There are also some variations to Knock Rummy. Some players impose a maximum count on the unmatched cards with which a player is allowed to knock. A popular figure is 15.

A version of the game often played in the UK restricts the knocker's options further. The knocker may not knock with more then one unmatched card. This requires him to have two three-card melds. Moreover, the unmatched card's rank cannot be above 3, so the knocker can go out only with a count of three, two or one. He is said to 'come up' for three, two or one (unless he goes rum, when he comes up for none). In this version, other players lay down their melds and can lay off onto the knocker's melds. The knocker has to pay the penalties given above if it turns out that another player has a lower count.

**Boathouse Rummy**  Boathouse Rummy is best for three to five players. The number of cards dealt to each player is nine minus the number of players.

A player on his turn has the option, as in the main game described above, of taking the top card of the discard pile or the top card of the stock, but if he takes the top card of the discard pile he must also take either the next card in the discard pile or the top card of the stock. He discards only one card, so by following this course he increases his hand by one card.

The Ace is either high or low, so can be in sequences of A, K, Q, or A, 2, 3. 'Round-the-corner' sequences are also allowed, making K, A, 2 a legitimate sequence.

Melds are not made during play, so a player goes out in one turn, and must discard when going out. The other players then lay down their melds and are debited with the values of their unmatched cards. In this version the Ace counts eleven rather than one. Cards cannot be laid off on other players melds, including the winner's.

**Continental Rummy** Continental Rummy is a game which had a vogue in the 1940s and is played with more than one pack. It is suitable for up to twelve players. If two to five play, two packs are used. If six to eight play, three packs are required. If nine to twelve play, four packs are necessary. Each pack must contain a Joker. All packs are shuffled together to form one pack.

Each player is dealt 15 cards, the remainder forming the stock. The procedure is as in the basic game, with players drawing either from the discard pile or the stock.

All melds are sequences – groups of cards of the same rank are not recognized. Jokers are wild cards and can represent whatever card their holders require. Players do not declare melds but keep them in their hands to go out on one turn. To go out, a player must have all his 15 cards melded, and his melds must conform to one of these patterns: five three-card sequences; three four-card sequences plus one of three cards; one five-card sequence, one four-card sequence and two three-card sequences. Since sequences of six or more can be split, this in effect covers all possible combinations.

The winner collects one unit from each player, plus two units for each Joker a losing player holds in his hand. A cumulative score can be kept by listing each player's debits, the winner being the player with the lowest total of debits when another player reaches, say, eleven.

**Kalookie** This game, also spelt Kaluki, is a two-pack rummy with some similarities to Canasta (not included in this book). It is for two to six players, and is played with two Canasta packs, ie two standard packs plus four Jokers (108 cards in all).

The number of cards dealt depends on the number of players. Two to four players receive 15 cards each; five players receive 13 cards; and six players receive eleven cards. Jokers count as wild cards.

The cards are valued thus: Joker 25 points, Ace eleven points, court cards ten points, other cards their pip value.

The play is as for the main game described, with the following differences:

i)   Ace counts high or low in sequences, ie A, K, Q and A, 2, 3 are sequences, but 'round-the-corner' sequences (K, A, 2) are not allowed.

ii) A group of three or four cards of the same rank may not contain duplicates, ie two cards of the same suit, two Jokers, or a Joker and a card of the suit it represents. In effect, this limits the number of cards in a group to four, with or without a Joker, since the Joker must represent one of the suits.

iii) Until he has melded, a player can take the top card of the discard pile only if he uses it in a meld, and then only if the meld, plus any other melds he might make at the same time, has a card value of 51. Until he can do this, therefore, a player on his turn may only draw from the stock. Once he has melded he can draw from the discard pile or the stock

iv) Until a player has melded, he cannot lay off cards to other players' melds.

v) Whether he has melded or not, a player on his turn may replace a Joker in another player's meld with a card which the Joker might be said to represent, taking the Joker into his own hand. For example in a meld of Joker, ♠4, ♣4, the Joker may legitimately be said to represent either ♦4 or ♥4, and a player holding either of these cards could, on his turn, exchange it for the Joker.

Play is otherwise as in the basic game, with players being debited for the unmatched cards held in their hands according to the values above.

# Scotch Whist

Scotch Whist is a strange game in that it is not Whist, and its connection with Scotland is unclear. It was first mentioned in a book published in New York in 1887. It is a simple but not unskilful game.

| | |
|---|---|
| **Alternative names** | Catch the Ten |
| **Players** | Four, playing in partnerships of two; two to eight for Variants |
| **Minimum age** | Twelve years old |
| **Skill factor** | A skilful game |
| **Special requirements** | Pen and paper for scoring |

### Aim
To win tricks containing scoring cards.

### Cards
The standard pack of 52 cards is used, from which are removed the 5s, 4s, 3s, and 2s, leaving a short pack of 36 cards.

The cards rank in 'plain suits' in the usual order, from Ace (high) to 6 (low), but in the trump suit the Jack is promoted above the Ace, so that the trump suit ranking is J, A, K, Q, 10, 9, 8, 7, 6.

### Preparation
Players draw from a spread pack to determine partners, the drawers of the two highest cards (Ace high) playing as partners against the other two. The highest card drawn indicates the first dealer. Partners sit opposite each other. The deal subsequently passes to the left.

The dealer deals the cards clockwise one at a time, face down, to each player, beginning with the 'eldest hand' (the player to the dealer's left) and continuing until all the cards have been dealt. The last card (the dealer's) is turned face up to indicate the trump card before being taken into the dealer's hand.

### Play
The eldest hand leads to the first trick; see p155 for an explanation of tricks and trick-taking. The normal rules of trick-taking apply: players must follow suit to the card led, and if they cannot may trump or discard as they wish. A trick is won by the highest trump it contains, or if there are no trumps by the highest card of the suit led. The winner of a trick leads to the next.

**Scoring** The scoring cards are the top five trumps and their values are:

| | |
|---|---|
| Jack | 11 points |
| 10 | 10 points |
| Ace | 4 points |
| King | 3 points |
| Queen | 2 points |

The holder of the Jack must win with it, as it is the highest trump, so the main object is to capture the 10, hence the alternative name for this game: Catch the Ten.

The side which captures the scoring cards in the trump suit scores their values as stated. In addition, the side which takes the majority of the tricks scores one point for every card captured over 18 (the number of cards in play being 36).

A running score is kept, and the first side to reach 41 points is the winner.

**Example hand**
The cards are dealt as shown, using the Bridge convention of calling the players North, South, East and West.

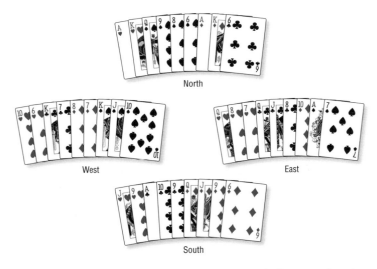

West dealt, so North leads. The last card dealt to the dealer was ♥6, so hearts are trumps. The play proceeds, with North leading his singleton:

| | North | East | South | West |
|---|---|---|---|---|
| 1 | ♣6 | ♣8 | ♣A | ♣7 |
| 2 | ♥A | ♣J | ♣9 | ♣K |

North

West

East

South

Scotch Whist

| | North | East | South | West |
|---|---|---|---|---|
| 3 | ♦A | ♦10 | ♦6 | ♦7 |
| 4 | ♠6 | ♠A | ♥J | ♠10 |
| 5 | ♠8 | ♣Q | ♣10 | ♦8 |
| 6 | ♠9 | ♠7 | ♦9 | ♠K |
| 7 | ♠Q | ♥7 | ♥9 | ♠J |
| 8 | ♦K | ♥Q | ♦J | ♥10 |
| 9 | ♥K | ♥8 | ♦Q | ♥6 |

As the cards lay, East/West did very well to make ten points for the ♥10, as North/South held the three top trumps. As it happened, East holding three trumps was crucial.

So North/South won 18 points for Jack, Ace, King of trumps, and East/West twelve for 10, Queen. North/South won the tricks six to three, so scored an extra six points (24 cards minus 18 = six points). After the first hand, North/South lead by 24 points to twelve.

### Variants

Two, three, five or seven people may play, with each player playing for himself. Six or eight may play with each playing for himself, or in partnerships of two, with partners sitting opposite each other.

The number of cards in the pack must be adjusted according to the number of players. If five or seven play the ♠6 is removed from the pack, and players receive seven cards each (five players) or five cards each (seven players). If eight play, the four 5s are added to the pack, making a pack of 40 cards, with each player receiving five.

With two, three or six players, the 36-card pack is used as in the basic game. With six players, each player receives six cards. If two or three play, the arrangement is slightly different. With two players, each player is dealt six cards face down one at a time, to form one hand, then six more one at a time to form a separate hand, then six more to form a third hand. The last card of all is turned up to indicate the trump suit for all three hands. The three hands are played separately. With three players, each is dealt two separate hands of six cards each.

No matter how many play, or how many hands the players have, the scores for taking the top five trumps in tricks are the same. The points scored for the majority of tricks are calculated by counting one point for each card won in tricks above the number the player (or the partnership) was dealt.

**French Whist** French Whist (again with no obvious connection to either Whist or France) is played in the same manner as Scotch Whist, with the addition of another value card. Ten points are awarded for winning the ♦10 (if diamonds are trumps the usual rules apply, ie there is not an extra ten points for winning the ♦10, which carries ten points for winning it anyway).

# Sequence

Sequence is the simplest form of the variety of games sometimes called stops games, of which Pope Joan is the ancestor and Newmarket the most modern form. It is a good game for young children learning to recognize the rank and sequence of playing cards.

| | |
|---|---|
| **Alternative names** | None, but Play or Pay is similar (see Variants) |
| **Players** | Three to ten; four to six is best |
| **Minimum age** | Six years old |
| **Skill factor** | Little skill needed |
| **Special requirements** | Pen and paper for scoring if a series of games is to be played |

## Aim
To be the first to get rid of all your cards.

## Cards
The standard pack of 52 cards is used, the cards ranking from 2 (low) to Ace (high).

## Preparation
Any player can pick up the cards, shuffle and deal them out one at a time face down to all players clockwise. It does not matter if some players get more cards than others. If a series of games is to be played, the deal passes to the left.

## Play
The 'eldest hand' (the player to the dealer's left) plays his lowest card to the table, announcing its rank and suit (if he has two or more equal lowest, he may choose which to play). The player who has the next highest card in the suit then plays it to the table and so on until whoever holds the Ace plays it, when the sequence ends. It does not matter if the same player plays two or more cards in a row (indeed this will often happen).

When the Ace is reached, he who played it must begin a new sequence by playing the lowest card in his hand, which might be in a new suit or might be in the same suit. Again players add to the card by playing the next highest until the Ace is reached again. However, if the card is of a suit that has been played before, the Ace will not be reached, and the sequence will stop at the point where the previous one began. Again, the player who plays the last card begins a new sequence with his lowest card.

The player who gets rid of all his cards first wins the hand, and if a series of games is being played each other player is given a penalty point for each card still in his hand. The winner is the player with the lowest number of penalty points when another player reaches an agreed maximum, say 12.

### Variants
**Play or Pay** This is a similar game. The difference is that any player starting a sequence may begin with any card he likes. The sequence does not end with Ace, but carries on with 2, eg the sequence will go Queen, King, Ace, 2, 3....etc. This is called a 'round-the-corner' sequence and means that all the cards in the suit will be played on the same sequence.

Each player begins the game with an equal pile of counters or matchsticks. The turn to play goes in rotation to the left. When a player plays a card to start a sequence, (eg ♥6) the player on his left must either play the next card in the sequence (♥7) or put a counter into the centre, as must the next, and so on until the next card (♥7) is played. Then the following player must play the next card (♥8) or put a counter into the centre and so on round the table. The player who gets rid of his cards first wins the counters from the centre, plus one counter from each other player according to how many cards in his hand.

The player with most counters when each player has dealt once is the winner. The problem with this game is the number of counters required – at least 20 for each player, and when many are playing it might be necessary halfway through the game to record how many counters each player has and then collect them all up to redistribute them all over again in order to finish the game.

Sequence is, for this and other reasons, recommended as the better game.

# Sixty-Six

Sixty-Six is an interesting traditional German game dating back to the 17th century. It has elements of Bezique and Pinochle (not included in this book) and is popular in Europe and the USA.

| | |
|---|---|
| **Alternative names** | None |
| **Players** | Two (see Variants for three and four players) |
| **Minimum age** | Twelve years old |
| **Skill factor** | Skill and a good memory are needed |
| **Special requirements** | Pen and paper for scoring |

## Aim
To score 66 or more points on a deal by winning tricks or declaring 'marriages', thus acquiring game points towards a total of seven needed to win.

## Cards
A shortened pack of 24 cards only is required, obtained by removing the 8s, 7s, 6s, 5s, 4s, 3s and 2s from a standard pack. Cards rank in the order A (high), 10, K, Q, J, 9 (low).

## Preparation
Players cut for deal, the cutter of the higher card (in the order listed above) being the first dealer. The deal thereafter alternates.

## Play
The dealer shuffles, the non-dealer cuts and the dealer deals six cards face down in two bundles of three to each player. The rest of the pack is turned face down in the centre to form a stock. The top card of the stock is turned over to denote the trump suit and it is placed face up at the foot of the stock and at right angles to it so that its suit and denomination can be read from the protruding end. The non-dealer then leads to the first trick; see p155 for an explanation of tricks and trick-taking. While any cards remain in the stock, the usual rules of trick-taking do not apply. The second player may play any card he likes – he is not required to follow suit, and may do so, or trump or discard as he pleases. A trick is won by the higher trump it contains, or if no trumps have been played, by the higher card in the suit led. The winner of a trick takes the top card from stock into his hand, and the loser the next card, so while the stock lasts, both hands are restored to six cards between tricks. The winner of the trick leads to the next.

The object at each deal is to score 66 or more points. One way of scoring is to win tricks containing point-scoring cards.

These cards, with their values, are:

| | |
|---|---|
| Each Ace | eleven points |
| Each 10 | ten points |
| Each King | four points |
| Each Queen | three points |
| Each Jack | two points |

Other ways to score points are by declaring marriages or taking the last trick. A marriage is a King and Queen of the same suit. A player may 'declare' a marriage only when it is his turn to lead. He does so by laying both cards face up on the table and leading one of them. The other card, although exposed, is still part of his hand and he may play it when he wishes. These additional scores are:

Royal Marriage (K, Q, of the trump suit): 40 points

Common marriage (K, Q, of a plain suit): 20 points

Bonus for winning the last trick: 10 points

If the non-dealer is dealt a marriage, he may declare it at once (and lead either card to the first trick) but he cannot score for it until he has won a trick.

Scores for marriages and last trick are entered on the scoresheet, but each player must keep a running total of his score from cards won in tricks in his head (the following sections headed Closing, Claiming and Scoring below explain why).

A player holding the 9 of trumps may exchange it for the turn-up card at any time after winning a trick and before leading to the next.

**End game** Unless the stock is closed (see below) the end game begins when the last two cards, including the upturned trump card, have been taken into the players' hands. The players play out their last six cards, but the rules change. Now players must follow suit to the card led if able, and only if they do not hold a card of the suit led may they trump or discard. Marriages can still be scored. As stated, the winner of the last trick scores ten points.

**Closing** At any time while cards remain in the stock a player, on his turn to lead, may announce he is closing, and turn over the trump card. He may do this either before or after drawing, so that each player's hand might contain five or six cards. Closing means that no further cards may be drawn from stock, and the players' hands are played out according to the rules described in End game above. Marriages may still be made, but no score can be claimed for last trick. A player who closes and doesn't win is penalized (see Scoring below).

**Claiming** At any time either player may announce during play that he has scored 66 points (this includes points made from marriages). No more tricks are played, and the players count their points. The claimant is penalized if he has failed to make 66 points (see Scoring below).

**Scoring** When the deal ends, either because the cards are all played or because a player has closed or claimed, each player counts the points he won by taking counting cards in his tricks, and adds them to the bonus points he has won from marriages or taking the last trick, if applicable.

If a player has closed the deal or claimed 66 points, and it is found that he has scored 66 points and his opponent has not, he scores one game point, or two game points if his opponent has fewer than 33 points (known as 'schneider') or three game points if his opponent has taken no tricks at all (known as 'schwarz'). If the opponent has also scored 66, however, neither player scores a game point, and an extra game point is added to the score of the winner of the following deal.

If a player closed the deal, or claimed 66 points, and it is found that he has not scored 66 points, then his opponent scores two points, or three if he has yet to win a trick.

If the deal is completed with neither player closing or claiming then a player who has 66 or more while his opponent has not scores a game point (or two if his opponent is 'schneidered' or three if his opponent is 'schwarzed'). Neither player scores if they both have more than 66 or tie on 65 (the number of points available discounting marriages is 130, so a tie at 65 is possible). If neither player scores, an extra game point is added to the score of the winner of the next deal.

The winner of the whole game is the first player to reach seven game points.

**Strategy** It is important for a player to keep a mental running total of the points he makes from winning tricks, and to claim the game when his total points (including any marriages he might declare) reaches 66. Otherwise his opponent might reach 66 as well, when he will lose the game point or points he might have won. Marriages score heavily, so players should hold on to Kings and Queens in the hope of drawing a card which completes a marriage. The only value in closing is to force the opponent to follow suit to the card led, so this tactic could be applied by a player who holds master trumps and possibly Aces in 'side suits', enabling him to pick up point-scoring cards from his opponent.

### Example hand
The hands are dealt as illustrated. The card turned up to indicate trumps is ♣10.

| Non-dealer | Dealer | Stock with trump indicator |
|---|---|---|

Play proceeds as follows, with the cards shown in brackets being the cards the two players drew from stock after the trick.

|   | Non-dealer | Dealer |
|---|---|---|
| 1 | ♠9 (♦Q) | ♠J (♥J) |

The non-dealer picks up ♦Q which gives him a marriage. He cannot declare it until he regains the lead.

| 2 | | |
|---|---|---|
| | ♣A (♥K) | ♥9 (♦10) |

The non-dealer decides to win with ♣A simply because he does not wish to part with any Kings or Queens and does not wish to give his opponent ten points by discarding ♠10, or eleven by discarding ♦A. As he has regained the lead he declares his marriage by laying down ♦K, Q before leading to trick 3.

| 3 | | |
|---|---|---|
| | ♦Q (♦9) | ♠10 (♣Q) |

The non-dealer has picked up another marriage with ♥K, and leads ♦Q. As we will see later this costs him the deal, where ♦A would quite probably have won it. The dealer takes the trick with ♦10 and draws from stock ♣Q, which gives him a royal marriage which he promptly declares. He has 55 points already and is thinking of closing or claiming shortly. He knows he can lead ♣K and ♣Q and probably win the next two tricks (as clubs are trumps and ♣A has been played and ♣10 is the turn-up card). This would bring him seven points (total 62) and he could pick up two or more from the non-dealer with these two tricks. Because we can see both hands we know that if the dealer leads ♥A he will win the trick and have 66 points, but the dealer fears that if he does this the non-dealer would trump (he does not know the non-dealer is trumpless, but he might guess so, as the non-dealer would probably have played a lower trump than Ace on trick 2 if he held one). He is in a good position to close, but plays cautiously.

The dealer timidly leads ♥J.

| 4 | | |
|---|---|---|
| | ♦9 (♣J) | ♥J (♠Q) |

The non-dealer could only win the trick by playing ♥K or ♥Q, which would deprive him of the marriage, so he discards ♦9 and hopes for the best. Alas for him, he drew the ♣J from stock one round too late. The dealer draws ♠Q and has another marriage, which he declares and scores 20 points. He also claims, and with 77 points to the non-dealer's 31 has scored 'schneider' and two game points.

## Variants

**Sixty-six for three players** The dealer does not deal any cards to himself and takes no part, the other two players playing as described above, with the 'eldest hand' (nearest to the dealer's left) taking the role of dealer as described. At the end of the deal, the actual dealer scores the same number of game points as the winner of the deal, and the deal passes to the left. If neither player wins, the dealer scores a game point, instead of an extra game point being carried forward to the next deal. The game is won, as in the parent game, by the first player to score seven game points, but the dealer is not allowed to win as the dealer. If the game points to be awarded to him bring his total to seven or more, his total remains at six and he must score his last point as an active player.

**Sixty-six for four players** The 8s and 7s are added to the usual pack, making a 32-card pack. Players play in partnerships, each player sitting opposite his partner. Each player is dealt eight cards, in bundles of three, three and two. The last card dealt is shown to the other players and indicates the trump suit before it is taken into the dealer's hand. There are no marriages, no closing and no claiming. Each hand is played out to the end.

The trick-taking rules are changed. Not only must every player follow suit if he can, he must also, if possible, play a higher card then any previously played to the trick. If a player cannot follow suit he must trump, if able, and if the trick already contains a trump he must overtrump if he can. This applies even if his partner holds the trick. The total number of points to be won remains at 130. A side scoring 66 to 99 scores one game point, 100 to 129 two game points, and 130 three game points. The winners are the first to seven game points.

# Slap-Jack

Slap-Jack is a hurly-burly party game for children, which is best played when there is a firm adult overseeing to prevent violence and tears. It is a game which should be played with one of those old packs consisting of 51 dog-eared cards, the other one having mysteriously disappeared many years ago, and which its owners cling onto in case the card should mysteriously appear again from under the settee: the sort of pack to be found in half the homes in the land.

| | |
|---:|:---|
| **Alternative names** | None |
| **Players** | Any reasonable number |
| **Minimum age** | Eight years old |
| **Skill factor** | Quick reactions needed |
| **Special requirements** | A table around which the players can gather and be within reach of the centre |

## Aim
To collect all the cards by touching the Jacks every time they appear.

## Cards
The standard pack of 52 cards is used, but it doesn't matter if any are missing.

## Preparation
Any player can pick up the cards and start dealing them, face down, one at a time to all players. Some will get more than others but it doesn't matter. All players arrange their cards in a face-down pile in front of them. They must not look at their cards.

## Play
Beginning with the 'eldest hand' (the player to the dealer's left), each player picks up the top card of his pile and plays it face up to a discard pile in the centre of the table. The player must not show the value of the card as he is playing it, but just turn it over as it is placed on top of the pile.

The other players must watch out for a Jack to be played. When a Jack is played, the first player to slap his hand on the pile wins all the cards in the pile. The player who lays the Jack can win the pile, but must take his hand away before he slaps the Jack. He cannot lay the Jack and slap it all in one movement.

This is where the adult referee comes in, because there will be disputes to sort out. It is a good idea to tell the players that when they slap the Jack they should leave their hand there. It makes it easier to decide whose hand is at the bottom.

If a player slaps a card which is not a Jack, that player must give the top card from his pile to the player who laid the card.

When a player wins the pile, he turns it over and adds it to his current pile, then shuffles the pile and sets it down before him ready to continue to play. The player to his left begins a new pile by turning over his top card and laying it on the table.

A player who loses all his cards has one more chance. He is out of the game unless he can slap the next Jack which appears after he lost his cards. If he manages to do this he picks up the pile and is in the game again, but if not he is out.

Eventually the players will be reduced to two, and the one who still has cards when the other player has laid all his is the winner.

# Snap

Snap is possibly the best-known of all children's card games. Commercial manufacturers have frequently dressed it up and published special cards for it, but it can be played as well, if not better, with ordinary playing cards.

| | |
|---|---|
| **Alternative names** | None |
| **Players** | Any reasonable number; two to six is best |
| **Minimum age** | Six years old |
| **Skill factor** | Quick reactions needed |
| **Special requirements** | None |

### Aim
To win all the cards in the pack.

### Cards
The standard pack of 52 cards is used, but as it is likely to get some hard treatment, it is best played with an old pack, and it doesn't matter if a card or two is missing.

### Preparation
Anybody may deal, as there is no advantage in it. The cards are dealt round face down in a clockwise direction, one at a time, to all players until the pack is exhausted. It does not matter that some players have more cards than others.

### Play
Players do not look at their cards, but square them up into a pile which each places face down on the table before him. The player to the left of the dealer begins the play by turning over the top card of his pile and placing it face up on the table beside his pile. The next player does the same and so on. As the play goes round and round the table, players on their turn take the top card from their face-down pack and turn it over onto what builds up into a face-up pile. Note that a player cannot win his own face-up pile by turning over a card which matches the top card of his own pile, since the turned-over card must go on top of the face-up pile and thus cover up the previous top card. Piles can only be won in pairs.

Every so often a player will turn a card onto his face-up pile which matches in rank the card on another player's face-up pile. When this happens any player may shout 'snap'. The first to do so wins all the cards in both piles and puts them face down underneath his own face-down pile.

After a successful call of 'snap', the player sitting to the left of the last player to turn over a card starts the game again by turning his next face-down card over to his face-up pile, and so on.

A player who has turned over all his face-down pile is not quite out of the game. While he has his face-up pile in front of him he can still call 'snap' and win himself another face-down pile. But if he loses his face-up pile, having already lost the face-down one, he must leave the game and await the next one.

If a player calls 'snap' when there are no cards on top of the face-up piles which match, that player must give a face-down card from his pile to each of the other players, beginning with the player to his left (in case there are not enough cards to go all the way round).

A game is hardly ever completed without a dispute about who called 'snap' first, so it is a good idea if there is an adult referee around to settle matters. Also, the referee should not allow players to turn over their cards in such a way that they get a good look at the card being turned over before the other players do.

The last player to have any cards left, and who therefore holds all the cards, is the winner.

### Variants
Some players play that all players turn their cards over onto a single central pile and 'snap' is called only when the two top cards are equal in rank. This is fine if there are only two or three players, but otherwise it gets a bit unruly.

Another variant is to allow a player whose face-down pile gets exhausted to turn his face-up pile over and resume, but this gets a little silly when there are only a few cards in the face-up pile and at every few turns the pile gets turned over.

# Snip-Snap-Snorem

Snip-Snap-Snorem, like other games now regarded as children's games, possibly arose from a simple gambling game. It can still be played for counters, if one wishes. It is a very old game with a possible reference to it dating back to the 18th century.

| | |
|---|---|
| **Alternative names** | Earl of Coventry (see Variants) |
| **Players** | Three or more |
| **Minimum age** | Six years old |
| **Skill factor** | No skill needed |
| **Special requirements** | None, but it can be played for counters |

## Aim
To get rid of all your cards.

## Cards
The standard pack of 52 cards is used.

## Preparation
Any player may pick up the cards, shuffle and begin to deal cards one at a time to each player round the table until a Jack appears. The player dealt the Jack becomes the first dealer. The deal subsequently passes to the left.

The dealer deals the cards clockwise one at a time, face down, until the pack is exhausted. It does not matter if some players receive a card more than others.

## Play
Players pick up their cards and examine their hands. The 'eldest hand' (the player to the dealer's left) begins play by leading any card he wishes face up to the table and announcing its rank. The player to his left must play to the table a card of equal rank, if able; if he cannot, he must pass. He cannot hold back a card if able to play.

The turn goes round the table clockwise until a player can play a second card of the rank led. As he plays it to the table, he says 'snip'. The turn passes until a third card of the rank is played, the player of it saying 'snap'. The turn passes until the fourth card of the rank is played with the announcement 'snorem'.

The player of 'snorem' picks up the four cards and discards them to one side face down. He then leads the first card of a new round by laying any card he likes and announcing its rank, and so on.

The player who first gets rid of all his cards is the winner.

## Variants

In the game described above, a player with two or more cards of the same rank plays them separately. Some players prefer that they are played at once, so that a player might, for example, play 'snip' and 'snap' together. This seems, however, to detract from the ceremonial nature of the game.

**Earl of Coventry** Earl of Coventry is exactly the same game as that described above, except for the announcements with the playing of the cards. Suppose the first card led is a 10. Its player says 'There's as good as 10 can be'. The player of the second card says 'There's a 10 as good as he'. The third player says 'There's the best of all the three' and the fourth says 'and there's the Earl of Coventry'.

**Playing for counters** When playing for counters (or coins), each player starts with a certain number of counters, say 20. A player who cannot go on his turn passes a counter to the last player who played a card. At the end of the game the player with most counters is the winner.

Alternatively, each player who announces 'snorem' collects a counter from each other player. Of course, players who can play a card must do so – it is illegal to pass while holding up a card for 'snorem'.

# Spade the Gardener

Spade the Gardener is of the family of children's games of which Go Fish is probably the best-known. Happy Families is a commercial game of the same type, with special cards. In fact, Spade the Gardener is almost the same game, but the fun comes with the names the children have to remember for each card. It is best if the children playing are of roughly the same age.

| | |
|---|---|
| **Alternative names** | None |
| **Players** | Three to eight, preferably of about the same age |
| **Minimum age** | Eight years old |
| **Skill factor** | A good memory is needed |
| **Special requirements** | None |

## Aim
To collect a 'family' of cards, a family being all the cards of a single suit.

## Cards
The standard pack of 52 cards is used. For up to five players, the 9s, 8s, 7s, 6s, 5s, 4s, 3s and 2s are removed, leaving a pack of 20 cards. For six players, the 9s are reinstated, while for seven or eight players the 8s are reinstated too. The cards rank from Ace (high) downwards.

## Preparation
Any player may pick up the cards, shuffle and begin to deal cards one at a time to each player round the table until a Jack appears. The player dealt the Jack becomes the first dealer. The deal subsequently passes to the left.

## Play
The first player to play is the one to the dealer's left, and he may ask any other player by name for a particular card. The only drawback is that he does not ask, for example, for the Queen of Spades, he asks for the family name, which in this case is Samuel Spade the Gardener's Wife. To get the card he must ask for it by the correct name. All the cards have a family name, as shown.

### The Spade Family

| Samuel | His wife | His son | His servant | His dog | His cat | His canary |

## The Spade Family

♠ K is Samuel Spade the Gardener

♠ Q is Samuel Spade the Gardener's Wife

♠ J is Samuel Spade the Gardener's Son

♠ A is Samuel Spade the Gardener's Servant

♠ 10 is Samuel Spade the Gardener's Dog

♠ 9 is Samuel Spade the Gardener's Cat

♠ 8 is Samuel Spade the Gardener's Canary

## The Heart Family

♥ K is Henry Heart the Butcher

♥ Q is Henry Heart the Butcher's Wife

♥ J is Henry Heart the Butcher's Son

♥ A is Henry Heart the Butcher's Servant

♥ 10 is Henry Heart the Butcher's Dog

♥ 9 is Henry Heart the Butcher's Cat

♥ 8 is Henry Heart the Butcher's Canary

## The Diamond Family

♦ K is Dominic Diamond the Jeweller

♦ Q is Dominic Diamond the Jeweller's Wife

♦ J is Dominic Diamond the Jeweller's Son

♦ A is Dominic Diamond the Jeweller's Servant

♦ 10 is Dominic Diamond the Jeweller's Dog

♦ 9 is Dominic Diamond the Jeweller's Cat

♦ 8 is Dominic Diamond the Jeweller's Canary

## The Club Family

♣ K is Clarence Club the Policeman

♣ Q is Clarence Club the Policeman's Wife

♣ J is Clarence Club the Policeman's Son

♣ A is Clarence Club the Policeman's Servant

♣ 10 is Clarence Club the Policeman's Dog

♣ 9 is Clarence Club the Policeman's Cat

♣ 8 is Clarence Club the Policeman's Canary

If a player uses the wrong name, for example instead of asking for 'Clarence Club the Policeman's Dog' he says by accident 'Have you got Clarence Club the Butcher's Dog?' or 'Samuel Club the Policeman's Dog', or even 'the ten of clubs', he gets nothing except, perhaps, laughed at. The turn passes to the next player. On the other hand, if he asks correctly for a card, and the player in question has it, then it must be handed to him. A player who receives a card thus may ask the same player, or another player, for a different card and may keep on asking for cards for as long as he gets them. He must name the player he is asking, to avoid confusion. When he meets with a refusal, his turn ends and the next player takes over.

A player can ask for any card, and need not have one of the family in his hand to ask for it. It follows that if a player asks for Samuel Spade the Gardener, and gets it, the next player on his turn can ask him for Samuel Spade the Gardener and he must hand it over again. Therefore it could take a long time for a player to get a whole family together. When he does, he lays them down on the table and continues in the game.

A player who runs out of cards, either because he has laid them down, or has had to give them to other players, or both, drops out of the game (but if he has laid down a family might still be a joint winner, because there are only four families in the whole game). The player who collects most families is the winner.

It can be a very frustrating game for young temperaments, especially when every time a child collects a few cards together towards a family, he is asked for them one by one and must give them up, so it is as well for a sympathetic adult to be on hand to preserve the peace.

# Stealing Bundles

Stealing Bundles is adapted from the Casino group of games and is a simplified version designed for children. Young children, though, are not very pleased when a bundle of three cards is stolen from them by a player with the fourth card.

| | |
|---|---|
| **Alternative names** | Old Man's Bundle, Stealing the Old Man's Bundle |
| **Players** | Two or four; better for four (as described below) |
| **Minimum age** | Seven years old |
| **Skill factor** | Little skill needed |
| **Special requirements** | Pen and paper for scoring if a series of games is to be played |

## Aim
To win as many completed 'bundles' (four cards of the same rank) as possible.

## Cards
The standard pack of 52 cards is used.

## Preparation
A dealer is selected by the players each drawing a card from a pack shuffled and spread on the table. The player who draws the highest card (Ace high, 2 low) is the first dealer. Thereafter the deal passes to the left.

## Play
The dealer shuffles, the player to his right cuts and the dealer, beginning with the player to his left, deals four face-down cards, one at a time to each player including himself. He then lays the next four cards face up in a row to the centre.

Players pick up their cards and the 'eldest hand' (the player to the dealer's left) begins play. If he has a card which matches in rank any of the four face-up cards, he captures it and lays the two cards face up in a pile in front of him. This is his first bundle. If two or three of the centre cards match one of his he can pick both or all three up for his first bundle.

He must play one card and one card only from his hand at each turn. If he cannot match any of the cards in the centre, he must add one of his cards to the centre. This is called 'trailing'.

Each player in turn then plays one of his cards, but as the game develops another option is open to him. Instead of capturing a matching card from the centre, a player may capture an opponent's bundle if he has a card which matches the rank of the cards in the bundle. A further option is to add a card to a bundle of his own.

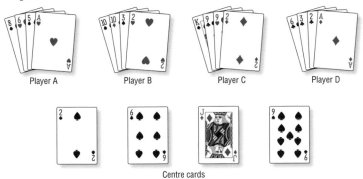

When the players have played all four of their cards the dealer deals each another four cards as before. The eldest hand resumes play. The dealer never replenishes the face-up cards in the centre, which are replaced by players trailing. The dealer will need to deal a third hand to the players before the deal ends. When a player completes a bundle of four cards he turns the pile face down before him.

The game ends when all the cards have been dealt and played. The winner is the player with the most bundles.

If a series of games is required, each player's number of bundles is recorded on a scoresheet, and the game can last for as many deals as required, provided all players deal an equal number. Two deals each, eight in all, makes a reasonable game for four players. Two players could play three deals each.

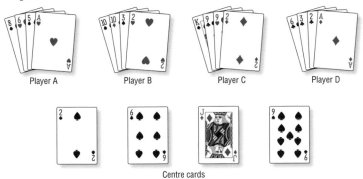

**Example hand**

Player A    Player B    Player C    Player D

Centre cards

The four hands are dealt as in the illustration. Player A is to play first. Play proceeds:

i)   Player A takes ♠6 matching it with ♥6 and laying the cards beside him in a bundle.

ii)  Player B matches ♠2 with ♥2 for a bundle.

iii) Player C matches ♠9 with ♣9 for a bundle. The ♥9 remains in his hand.

iv)  Player D steals Player A's bundle of 6s with his ♣6 making a bundle of three 6s.

v)   Player A cannot capture a card from the centre, or a bundle, and trails ♥A, playing it to the centre.

vi)  Player B cannot capture and trails ♠10.

vii) Player C plays ♥9 to his bundle.

viii) Player D captures ♥A with ♦A for a second bundle.

ix) Player A trails ♠8 to the centre.

x) Player B captures ♠10 with ♦10 for a bundle.

xi) Player C steals Player B's bundle of 2s with ♦2, making a bundle of three cards.

xii) Player D steals Player C's bundle of 2s with ♣2, to complete the bundle of four 2s, which he lays in a face-down pile before him.

xiii) Player A trails ♠5.

xiv) Player B trails ♠3.

xv) Player C trails ♠K.

xvi) Player D captures ♠3 with ♣3 to begin a bundle of 3s.

So at the end of the first round, there are again four cards in the centre (as seen the number in the centre varies). Player D has won the first complete bundle. Player B has a bundle of two 10s, Player C of three 9s and Player D of three 6s, two Aces and two 3s.

It should be noted that holding bundles of two or three cards is no advantage. For example, whoever is dealt the fourth 6 in the Example Hand will capture Player D's three 6s, and Player D has no better prospect of a complete bundle of 6s than any other player.

Now that the players have played all their cards, the dealer deals a second hand of four cards to each as before, and play continues.

# Switch

Switch is a general name for a game which goes by many others, including Swedish Rummy, a misleading name which probably originated in the USA. The game is not Swedish and nothing like Rummy. In the version described, Jacks are wild cards, and the game is also called Crazy Jacks. In some versions other cards are wild, leading to names like Crazy Aces or Crazy Eights for what is virtually the same game. Rules vary everywhere.

| | |
|---:|:---|
| **Alternative names** | Black Jack, Crazy Jacks, Swedish Rummy |
| **Players** | Two to six, with four or five best |
| **Minimum age** | Ten years old |
| **Skill factor** | Some skill needed |
| **Special requirements** | Pen and paper for scoring |

## Aim
To get rid of all your cards.

## Cards
The standard pack of 52 cards is used, the cards ranking from Ace (high) to 2 (low).

## Preparation
Any player may pick up the cards, shuffle and begin to deal cards one at a time to each player round the table until a Jack appears. The player dealt the Jack becomes the first dealer.

The dealer deals the cards one at a time to each player, face down. If two to four people play each player is dealt seven cards; if five or six play each receives five cards. The remainder of the cards are placed in the centre of the table face down to provide a 'stock'.

## Play
The 'eldest hand' (the player to the dealer's left) plays any card he wishes to a discard pile in the centre, and the player to his left must play a card of the same suit or rank upon it. If he cannot, he must draw the top card of the stock, and continue to do so until he draws a card which will enable him to discard it to the centre. Play proceeds in this way, but some ranks of cards have special properties as follows:

*Jacks*    A Jack is a wild card and can be played at any time. Furthermore, the player of a Jack can change the suit to the suit of his choice.

*Deuces*    When a player plays a 2, which also can be played at any time, the following player, unless he can play a 2, must take two cards from the stock and forgo his opportunity to discard. However, if he can play a 2, the following player, facing two consecutive 2s, must either play a 2 himself or draw four cards from the stock without discarding any. A third consecutive 2 forces the following player to draw six cards, and four consecutive 2s forces the next player to draw eight.

*Treys*  The play of a 3, which also can be played at any time, operates like the 2. The following player, unless he can play a 3, must take three cards from stock without discarding, and successive 3s force a player to take six, nine or twelve cards from the stock.

*Kings*  The play of a King, which must be of the correct prevailing suit, reverses the order of play from clockwise to anti-clockwise. Of course, the play of a second King reverses it back to normal again.

*Eights*  The play of an 8, which must be of the correct suit, forces the following player to miss a turn.

When the stock is exhausted, play continues with a player unable to play a legitimate card merely missing a turn.

The player to get rid of his cards first and go out is the winner of the deal.

The ranks of special significance in Switch

**Scoring** When a player goes out, each of the others is debited with the cards held in his hand. Jacks count as 15, Aces eleven, court cards as ten and other cards at their pip value. Scores are kept, and when one player's debit score reaches 100, the player with the lowest debit score is the winner.

# Thirty-One

Thirty-One is a number that often crops up in gambling games (eg **Trente et Quarante**, still played in casinos), but the game now known as **Thirty-One** is usually a watered-down version of the game described below designed for younger players. The gambling version is played for a pool.

| | |
|---|---|
| **Alternative names** | Schnautz, Trente-et-Un |
| **Players** | Three to fifteen (the more the better) |
| **Minimum age** | Ten years old |
| **Skill factor** | Some judgement needed |
| **Special requirements** | Cash, chips or counters for staking; a bowl or saucer to hold the pool of stakes |

### Aim

To hold or build a hand of three cards of the same suit with a higher point count than the hands of other players.

### Cards

The standard pack of 52 cards is used. Aces count eleven points, court cards ten points and other cards their pip value. If necessary to break a tie, Ace, King, Queen, Jack rank in that order.

### Preparation

Before each deal the amount to be put into the pool by all players must be agreed. The first dealer is decided by each player drawing a card from a spread pack; the highest drawer (Ace high, 2 low) becoming the first dealer. The deal passes to the left after each deal. The dealer takes part as a normal player, there being no advantage to the dealer in the game. In fact there is a slight disadvantage, as he is last to draw from the 'widow' (the extra hand). Therefore the game should not end before all players have dealt an equal number of times.

The cards are shuffled (the dealer having the right to shuffle last) and the player to the right of the dealer cuts.

### Play

The dealer deals cards clockwise one at a time face down to each player beginning with the 'eldest hand' (the player to his left) and one face up to a widow in the centre of the table, until each player and the widow has three cards.

Each player examines his cards and announces it immediately if he holds one of three combinations:

i) Three cards of one suit with a points count of 31 (this can be only an Ace with any two cards from the four ranks which count ten (K, Q, J, 10). He announces '31 points'.

ii) Any three cards of the same rank. This hand is valued at 30½ points, so beats any hand except (i) above. He announces 'three cards'.

iii) Three cards of one suit not totalling 31 points, but which he thinks has a points total sufficient to win, ie a higher points total than any other player. He announces his points total.

When a player announces immediately, there is no further play. All players expose their hands and the highest hand wins the pool. Where there is a tie, the hand holding the highest ranking card wins, the cards ranking Ace, King, Queen, Jack, ... 2. If equal, the next highest card decides and if again equal, the third. Only if two or more hands are identical is the pool shared.

When no player announces immediately, an exchange of cards begins. Beginning with the eldest hand, each player must exchange one card with the widow. Play continues like this for as many rounds as necessary and a player may, if he wishes, take from the widow a card he previously discarded.

Play continues, with each player trying to improve his hand, of course, until a player has 31 points or is satisfied with his hand. If he has 31 he must announce it immediately. He cannot be beaten and he takes the pool.

If a player has a count he is satisfied with, on his next turn he knocks on the table rather than exchanging a card with the widow (note he cannot knock on the same turn as he exchanges a card). When a player knocks, play continues once round the table until it reaches the knocker. On this last round, players are not forced to exchange a card with the widow – they are allowed to pass.

When the turn reaches the knocker, all players then expose their hands, and the player with the highest count in one suit wins the pool.

Since a player cannot knock without having three cards of the same suit or the same rank, it can happen that the game continues too long without anybody knocking. It is suggested that if there are ten rounds of players exchanging a card without anybody knocking, the hand should be abandoned. The pool remains, the deal passes as usual, and players contribute to the pool as usual, so that the next game has a double pool.

**Strategy** Players with any count (ie players with three cards of the same suit) should always consider the possibility of knocking. A count of 25 or so often wins, particularly if dealt initially, when no players have had a chance to exchange cards with the widow. When several rounds of exchanges have been made and the cards in the widow are of low denomination, an even lower count might be worth knocking with – certainly a better option than allowing the hand to be abandoned.

# Twenty-Nine

Twenty-Nine is an interesting adding-up game which all the family can play. It is useful for getting young children familiar with addition.

| | |
|---|---|
| **Alternative names** | None |
| **Players** | Two to six |
| **Minimum age** | Seven years old |
| **Skill factor** | Little skill needed |
| **Special requirements** | Pen and paper for scoring if a series of games is to be played |

## Aim
To bring the pip value of a pile of cards to exactly 29, thus winning the pile. Ultimately the aim is to win the most cards.

## Cards
The standard pack of 52 cards is used from which as many 10s are removed to allow all players to have the same number of cards. Thus two and four players play with the full pack; with three players one 10 is dropped, with five players two 10s are dropped and with six players all four 10s are dropped. For the purposes of counting, all cards have a value. All Aces and court cards count one each and all other cards their pip values.

## Preparation
From a pack which has been spread face down each player chooses a card. He who draws the highest (for this purpose cards rank conventionally: Aces are high and 2s low) is the first dealer. Thereafter the deal passes to the left.

## Play
The dealer shuffles, the player to his right cuts, and the dealer deals all the cards face down one at a time to each player clockwise to his left.

The 'eldest hand' (the player to the dealer's left) leads any card to the table, announcing its value as set out above. The next player in turn adds a card to it announcing the combined value, and succeeding players add to the pile in the same manner.

The object is to bring the total value of the pile to exactly 29. A player who achieves this collects all the cards in the pile and places them face down before him, and the player to his left begins a new pile by playing any card in his hand.

A player who cannot play a card without bringing the total of the pile to more than 29 misses his turn. Play continues until all the cards have been played.

With two or four players the cards will run out to coincide with the last pile reaching 29 (there being eight x 29 points in the pack). With other numbers of players, the last pile will not reach 29. It is won by the last player to play a card to it.

When all players' hands are exhausted, players count the number of cards they have won, the player with the most being the winner of the hand. If a series of games is wanted, each player's score should be kept on a scoresheet and the player with most cards won after an agreed number of deals is the winner.

It is suggested that with two or three players, four deals each should constitute a game; with four or five players, three deals each and with six players, two deals each.

### Variants

This game lends itself to partnership play, with four players making two partnerships of two, and six players three partnerships of two. Partners sit opposite each other.

# War

War is one of the simplest games in this book. Despite its name it is not aggressive and two people can play amicably for a long time. For some it lasts too long, but others find it an agreeable way of gently passing half an hour or so without the need to trouble the brainbox. Shorter versions are suggested under Variants.

| | |
|---|---|
| **Alternative names** | Battle (see Variants) |
| **Players** | Two |
| **Minimum age** | Six years old |
| **Skill factor** | No skill needed |
| **Special requirements** | None |

### Aim
To win all the cards.

### Cards
The standard pack of 52 cards is used, the cards ranking from Ace (high) to 2 (low).

### Preparation
None, as it doesn't matter who deals or leads.

### Play
Either player can pick up the cards, shuffle them and deal one at a time to both players.

The players do not look at their cards but keep them in a neat pile face down in front of them.

Each player turns over his first card and puts it in the centre face up. The player who puts in the higher card by rank wins both (suits are immaterial) and places both cards face down at the bottom of his pile.

It is only if the two cards are of equal rank that a slight deviation from the norm disturbs the tranquil atmosphere. In this case each player lays a card face down on top of his first card, followed by another card face up. Whoever lays the higher card of these last two wins all six cards, and places them (taking care to make sure they are all face down) on the bottom of his pile. Should the second face up cards in the pile be also equal, then the nearest this game gets to pandemonium breaks out, as the players now must play another face-down card on the pile followed by another face up. And so on, if the heart can stand the strain.

Eventually one player will take all the cards and be an exhausted winner.

### Variants

If the game takes longer than desired, a shorter version can be played merely by using a shorter pack, such as the 40-card pack (minus all the court cards) or the 32-card pack (minus all the ranks from 2 to 6).

**Battle** This is really the same game with some of the excitement removed. If there is a tie with the pair of cards played the two cards are merely put aside and taken by the winner of the next pair.

# More About
# Playing Cards

# Card Games Basics

There are certain basic facts, rules and customs which apply to all card games.

### The pack
The standard pack consists of 52 cards containing four suits, each identified by a symbol: spades (♠), hearts (♥), diamonds (♦) and clubs (♣). Hearts and diamonds are printed in red, spades and clubs in black. There are 13 cards in each suit, each having a rank: Ace (A), King (K), Queen (Q), Jack (J), 10, 9, 8, 7, 6, 5, 4, 3, 2. When buying a pack, it is usual to find two additional cards called Jokers, often illustrated with a figure dressed as a court jester, with cap and bells. The Jokers are rarely used but have been added to the pack specially for a few games.

Some games require two or more packs, and some, particularly games which originate from Spain, Italy, Germany or Switzerland, require a 'short pack', which is formed from the standard pack by removing the lower ranking cards: for a 40-card pack, the 4s, 3s and 2s are removed; for a 36-card pack, the 5s are also removed; for a 32-card pack, the 6s are also removed.

The suits in most games are of equal value, but some games grade the suits in order of importance. So far as the ranks of individual cards are concerned, in most games the cards are ranked in importance as above, with the Ace the highest ranked. Originally, the Ace was the one and ranked lowest, but early in the history of card games (ie before 1500) the Ace began to take precedence over all others. In some games, however, the old order stands, and Ace counts as the lowest card. Some games, especially those which originate in continental Europe, have eccentric rankings of the cards, particularly regarding 10s and 2s. Rankings are given, where appropriate, in the descriptions of all the games in the main text.

### Deciding partnerships
In games of four players requiring partnerships, respective partners can be decided by mutual agreement or by chance. If by chance is preferred, the usual method is for any player to shuffle the cards and another to cut (see Shuffling and Cutting, below). Each player then cuts the pack, with the two players cutting the lowest cards forming a partnership against the two highest. The lowest of all is the dealer and he chooses his seat with his partner sitting opposite. Any variations from this practice are mentioned in the individual descriptions of games.

### Rotation of play
In most games the right to deal, the order of bidding (if any) and the turn to play rotate to the left, ie clockwise. However, in some games originating in continental Europe the converse is true, and play rotates to the right, ie anti-clockwise.

### Shuffling
A safe way to shuffle the pack is to place it on the table, and divide it roughly into two by taking the top half and placing it end to end with the lower half, as in the first illustration.

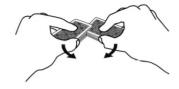

Then, holding the two halves abutting each other, riffle them together by running the thumbs up the sides of each half while holding the two packs firm with the fingers on the opposite edge, as shown in the second illustration. With the two halves interleaved, slide them together as in the third illustration. Then, take about a third of the cards from the top and place the bottom two-thirds on top of them. Repeat the whole process twice more, not forgetting the final cut, and the pack should be well shuffled.

## Cutting

There are two types of cut. In the cut whereby each player cuts the pack to determine partners or who deals, the player merely takes a packet of cards from the top of the pack, which should be face down on the table, and turns it over to expose the bottom card.

The cut made before another player deals has another purpose. It is the final insurance that the pack has not been arranged. In this cut, the player takes a packet from the top of the face-down pack (the packet should be of at least five cards), places it on the table face down and places what was previously the lower part of the pack on top of it.

## Dealing

It is customary before the deal for the pack to be shuffled by the dealer. Although any player may ask to shuffle prior to the dealer, the dealer has the right to shuffle last. He then places the pack face down before his right-hand neighbour, who cuts it as described above. It is in order for this player merely to take a packet from the top of the pack and place it on the table, leaving the dealer to complete the cut by placing the lower portion on top. It is open for a player to refuse to cut, in which case any other player may volunteer. If none wishes to, the dealer must cut the cards himself. This description is for games where the play rotates to the left; in games where play rotates anti-clockwise, the left-hand neighbour of the dealer cuts.

The dealer deals the cards, in nearly all games face down, to each player in turn, either one at a time or in packets as the game requires, until all players have the required number. It is customary and courteous for players to wait until the deal is complete before touching their cards.

## Misdealing

If there is a misdeal, which can occur for various reasons, such as a card being turned face up, or being already face up in the pack, or there being cards missing, the cards must be gathered up and the dealer must begin again. However, if there is an advantage in being the dealer, then the misdealer loses the deal, which passes to the next player.

## Trumps and tricks

Many games involve taking 'tricks'. A trick is a round of play to which each player contributes a card. The usual rule (and one must emphasize the *usual* rule) is that all players must follow suit to the card led, eg if the leader (the player who contributes the first card to the trick) leads a heart, all other players must contribute a heart if they are able to, ie if they hold a heart in their hand. If a player does not hold a card of the suit led, he must play any other card. The card which wins the trick is the highest card that it contains of the suit led.

However, in most trick-taking games, there is a 'trump' suit, which is decided by various different methods according to the rules of the game being played. The word 'trump' is a corruption of 'triumph', and a card from the trump suit triumphs over one from any other suit. Thus, where there is a trump suit, a player who does not hold a card of the suit led, but who does hold a card of the trump suit, may play the trump, which will win the trick, unless a subsequent player who is also devoid of a card in the suit led plays a higher trump. Thus, a trick is won by the highest trump it contains, or if it does not contain a trump, by the highest card in the suit led.

A player's first obligation is to play a card in the suit led. If he is unable to, he may play a trump, thus beating all cards of the suit led. He is not allowed to play a trump if he holds a card of the suit led. On the other hand, if he does not hold a card of the suit led, he is not obliged to play a trump – he may play any other card (called a 'discard'). A discard, of course, can never win a trick. A player is not obliged to try to win a trick.

To sum up: the leader plays a card of a certain suit (which may or may not be a trump). Subsequent players must follow suit if they can, and if they cannot may play a trump or discard as they wish. The highest trump wins the trick – if none is played the highest card of the suit led wins.

This is what is meant by the phrase often used in this book: 'the normal rules of trick-taking apply'.

Of course, inevitably there are games where the normal rules do not apply. In these games it might be compulsory to trump, or it might be that you can trump even if holding a card of the suit led, or it might even be that it is not obligatory to follow suit to the card led. In all games where these deviations from the normal rules apply they are carefully explained in the individual descriptions of play.

## Duration of play
It is advisable, and important in games where money is changing hands, to agree a time when play will stop, or at least a time when any player who wishes to leave the game may do so. This saves a lot of hard feeling in games where players who are winning feel obliged to play for longer than they wish because losing players insist on nobody leaving while they themselves are losing.

# Card Games Glossary

The glossary does not include game names or variants, for which the index can be consulted.

**auction** the period in which bidding takes place

**bank** an amount of chips or coins put up by a banker for players to bet against

**banker** a person who keeps or acts as the bank

**barter** in Trade or Barter, to offer a face-down card to the player on one's left, which he may accept or not

**baulking** in Cribbage, the practice by the non-dealer of laying away cards to the crib from which it is difficult to score points

**bid** an offer to make a certain number of tricks or points in play

*bidding* the act or process of making bids, or the bids made

**blind dog's chance** in Knockout Whist a final chance offered to a player to continue in the game when he has been knocked out for a second time having already been given a second chance

**book** in Pelmanism and Pig, a set of all four cards of the same rank

**box** in Cribbage, *same as* crib

**build** (*a*) in patience games, to transfer cards to foundations or to other cards in the tableau (*b*) in Casino, to play a card to the layout which will allow a card or cards to be captured on a future turn

*multiple build* in Casino, an attempt to capture several cards in a future turn by making more than one build at a time

*single build* in Casino, an attempt to capture two or more cards in a future turn by building

**bundle** in Stealing Bundles, a set of two or more cards of the same rank; a completed bundle is the set of all four cards of a rank

**bust** (*a*) in Pontoon, to exceed the score of 21 when drawing cards (*b*) in Farmer, to exceed the score of 16 when drawing cards

**buy** in Pontoon, to receive a card face down, for a stake not exceeding the original stake

**capture** to win possession of a card during play, thus taking it into the hand or scoring points from it

**card** one of a pack, usually of 52 cards, divided into four suits used in playing games

*boodle card* a card on which coins or chips are placed which can be won by players

*court card* the King, Queen or Jack of each suit

*plain card* a card other than a court card

*trump card* a card turned up to determine the trump suit; any card of that suit, or a card otherwise designated a trump by the rules of the game

**chip** a token of wood, plastic or similar, used to represent money

**claiming** in Sixty-Six, an announcement by a player that he has a winning score of 66 points or more, which brings play to an end

**closing** in Sixty-Six, an announcement by a player that the hand is to be played out without further cards being drawn from stock

**clubs** (♣) one of the four customary suits of playing cards, comprising 13 cards with black trefoil pips

**colour** the colour of the pips and characters on a card: red for diamonds and hearts, black for spades and clubs

**combining** in Casino, a way of capturing two or more cards by playing a card the pip total of which equals the sum of the pip totals of the cards

**come up** in forms of Rummy where a player can go out without melding all of his cards, he is said to 'come up' for the pip value of the unmelded card, eg he might 'come up for two'

**contract** an undertaking by a player or partnership to win a certain number of tricks

**crib** in Cribbage, the extra hand formed by the players' discards

**cucumbered** in Cucumber, to reach a total of 30 penalty points, and thus be forced to drop out of the game

**cut** to divide a pack of cards by lifting the upper portion at random, either to expose a card or suit, or in order to replace the parts of the pack in a different order before dealing

**dead hand** an extra hand which plays no part in a game

**deadwood** in Rummy, the unmelded cards remaining in players' hands after a player has gone out and other cards have been laid off where possible

**deal** (*a*) to distribute cards to each player, or the act of distributing cards (*b*) the period between one deal and the next, including bidding, playing, scoring etc

*dealer* a person who deals cards, or whose turn it is to deal, or who has dealt the hand in play

**deck** *same as* pack

**declare** to show cards in order to score

**deuce** the 2 of each suit

**diamonds** (♦) one of the four customary suits of playing cards, comprising 13 cards with red diamond-shaped pips

**discard** to throw away a card or cards, as not needed or not allowed by the game; to throw down a (useless) card of another suit when you cannot follow suit and cannot or will not trump; the act of discarding; the card or cards thrown out of the hand

**dog's chance, dog's life** in Knockout Whist, a second chance offered to a player who would otherwise be knocked out of the game

**down** in Sergeant Major the status of a player who takes fewer tricks than his target, and who thus is obliged on the next deal to exchange a good card for an inferior one from an 'up' player

**draw** (*a*) to take a card from a face-down pack to determine seats, dealer etc (*b*) to take a card or cards from the stock, either to replace discards or to increase the number of cards held

**drop out** to cease to play any part in a game, either by choice or necessity

**elder, eldest hand** the player on the dealer's left (or, in games of Spanish derivation, the player on the dealer's right)

**expose** to show the cards in a hand to other players or the banker

**face** the printed side of a playing card that shows its pip value, as opposed to the back

*face down* with the side of the card that displays the pip value hidden

*face up* with the side of the card that displays the pip value visible

**fan** cards arranged in a crescent shape, usually with each card slightly overlapping another

**farmer** in Farmer, the dealer

**foundation** in patience games, a card which is separated from the pack or tableau and upon which a whole suit or sequence must be built

**get out** to win a patience game by achieving the aim of the game

**go** in Cribbage, an announcement that a player cannot play without exceeding 31; the score for an opponent's failure to play

*go out* to win by getting rid of all the cards in a hand

*go rummy* in Rummy, to meld all the cards held and go out in one turn, without having previously melded

**hand** the set of cards held by a player at one deal; the play of a single deal of cards

**hearts** (♥) one of the four customary suits of playing cards, comprising 13 cards with red heart-shaped pips

**heel** *same as* talon

**his nob** in Cribbage, a point scored for holding the Jack of the same suit as the start

**hitting the moon** in Omnibus Hearts, the scoring of 26 points by a player who takes all fifteen counting cards

**Joker** a 53rd or 54th card in the pack, used in some games

**Jubilee numbers** in Jubilee, a number which

is a multiple of 25, and to which the players attempt to bring the pip total of the central pile of cards, thus scoring points

**kitty** *same as* pool

**knave** a Jack

**knock** *(a)* in Rummy, to signify the end of the deal by laying down your hand, sometimes accompanied by knocking on the table *(b)* in Golf, to indicate by tapping on the table that the deal will end when it is next your turn to play, whereupon all players must expose their hands

**lay off** in Rummy, to add cards to a meld already on the table

**layout** the arrangement of cards upon the table, especially in patience games

**lead** to play the first card of a round or trick; the first card laid

**make** to declare as trumps; to win a trick

**marriage** in Sixty-Six, a scoring combination of a King and a Queen of the same suit

*common marriage* a King and a Queen of a plain suit

*royal marriage* a King and a Queen of the trump suit

**meld** a combination or group of scoring cards, usually three or more of the same rank, or of the same suit and in sequence; to show or announce such a group

**muggins** in Cribbage, a call by which, if a player overlooks points when scoring, his opponent can claim the points for himself

**non-dealer** in a two-handed game, the player who is not currently acting as the dealer

**obstacle** in Obstacle Race, one of the numbers (eg 55, 66) to which players attempt to bring the pip total of the central pile of cards, thus scoring a point

**old maid** in Old Maid, the losing player who holds the odd Queen at the end of the game

**pack** a complete set of playing cards, usually comprising 52 cards

**pair** two cards of the same rank

*pairing* in Casino, a way of capturing a card by matching it to a card of the same rank already held

**partnership** a team of two, or occasionally more, players

**pass** to abstain from making a bid, declaration or other play

**patience** a card game for one (called 'solitaire' in North America)

**pegging** in Cribbage, the scoring during the first part of the game, and the keeping of the score by moving pegs round the Cribbage board

**pip** a suit symbol spot on a card

*pip value* the total of the pips on a playing card, for example a 3 card has a pip value of 3

**point** in Commerce, the total points value of two or three cards of the same suit

**pontoon** in Pontoon, a two-card hand of 21, consisting of an Ace and a 10-count card

**pool** the collective stakes of a number of players, which can be won during the game

*scoop the pool* to win the total amount of money in the pool

**prial** in Pontoon, a hand of three '/s

**rams** in Rams, an undertaking by the declarer to win all five tricks

**rank** the grade or position of a particular card in its suit, for example 3, 10 or Jack are ranks

**round-the-corner** applied to a continuous sequence of cards in which the Ace counts both high and low, ie one running highest to lowest as in Queen, King, Ace, 2, 3 and so on

**rum hand** in Rummy, a hand in which all the cards are melded

**schneider** in Sixty-Six, to restrict the opponent to fewer than 33 points

*schneidered* in Sixty-Six, applied to a player who fails to score 33 points

**schwarz** in Sixty-Six, a win in which the opponent does not score a point

*schwarzed* in Sixty-Six, applied to an opponent who fails to score a point

**sequence** a set of three or more cards consecutive in value

*ascending sequence* a sequence in which cards run up, for example from 2 to King

*descending sequence* a sequence in

which cards run down, for example from King to 2

**short pack, shortened pack** a pack which has been reduced from 52 cards to some other number by the removal of all cards of a certain rank or ranks

**show** in Cribbage, the second part of play

**shuffle** to mix cards at random

**slam** in Omnibus Hearts, the same as hitting the moon

**spades (♠)** (a) one of the four customary suits of playing cards, comprising 13 cards with black shovel-like pips (b) in Casino, a point won for capturing the majority of the spades

**stake** money or chips staked on an outcome not yet known; to deposit as a wager

**maximum stake** the highest amount of coins and chips which players may contribute in a gambling game

**minimum stake** the lowest amount of coins and chips which players are obliged to contribute in a gambling game

**stand** *same as* stick

**start** in Cribbage, the top card of the lower half of the cut pack, which is revealed by the dealer and placed face up on the top of the reunited pack

**stick** (a) in Pontoon, a declaration that a player is happy with his count and will not take any more cards (b) in Farmer, a declaration that a player will not take any more cards, either because he is happy with his count, or because he has bust (he must not say which)

**stock** the undealt part of a pack of cards, which may be used later in the deal

**stop** in Newmarket, an interruption of play caused by the required next card in the sequence not being in play

**suit** one of the sets of cards of the same denomination: clubs, diamonds, hearts or spades

**follow suit** to play a card of the same suit as the one which was led

**plain suit** a suit other than the trump suit

**side suit** *same as* plain suit

**trump suit** a suit that ranks higher than any other suit

**sweep** in Casino, the taking of all the cards in the layout at once; the score for this

**tableau** in patience games, the main part of the layout of cards on the table

**take-all** in Omnibus Hearts, *same as* hitting the moon

**talon** in patience games, a waste pile; cards laid aside as unplayable when turned up from stock, but which are available for play later

**trade** in Trade or Barter, to buy a new card from the dealer

**trailing** (a) in Casino, the adding of a card from a player's hand to the layout when unable to build or take in (b) in Stealing Bundles, the adding of a player's card to the centre, when he cannot match any of the cards currently in the centre

**trey** the three of each suit

**trick** a round of play at cards, in which each player contributes one card; the cards so played and taken by the winner

**overtrick** a trick in excess of the number specified in a contract

**triplet** in Commerce, three cards of the same rank

**trump, trumps** a suit that ranks higher than any other suit, so that any card of this suit ranks higher than any card of the other three suits; a card of this suit; to play a trump card instead of following suit

**twist** in Pontoon, the option for a player to receive a further card face up, for which he does not pay

**two for his heels** in Cribbage, two points scored by the dealer when a Jack is turned up as the start

**up** in Sergeant Major, the status of a player who takes more tricks than his target, and who thus is entitled on the next deal to exchange a card or cards for superior ones of the same suit with a 'down' player

**void** the total absence of cards of a particular suit in a hand

**widow** an extra hand

# Court Cards

' "Off with her head!" the Queen shouted at the top of her voice. Nobody moved.

"Who cares for *you*?" said Alice... "You're nothing but a pack of cards!" '

Lewis Carroll, *Alice's Adventures in Wonderland*

Since the days of Alice, the home computer has added millions to the number of people who play cards. That is if manipulating images on a screen by means of a mouse can be called 'playing cards'.

Playing with real people and handling real cards is surely more satisfying. Alice found in Wonderland that the cards themselves for a time became real people. And in a sense they are.

Court cards manufactured in France carried the names of real kings, queens and knights from as early as the 1500s. The names occasionally changed, or switched suits, but not by much. The generally accepted identities of those monarchs and their courts who are dealt to us whenever we play cards were well established by the time a representative pack was issued in Paris in 1760.

In this pack, the Queen of hearts, famous in *Alice* for chopping off the heads of all who crossed her, is named as Judith, the heroine of one of the apocryphal books of the Bible. She was the widow of the Jew Manasseh, and she seduced the conquering Assyrian general, Holofernes, taking the opportunity to chop off his head in his own tent, thus saving Israel from destruction. Clearly the Reverend Charles Dodgson, who used the pen name Lewis Carroll, knew all about Judith's reincarnation as the Queen of hearts when he invented the playing card story for his young friend Alice.

Judith's card consort, the King of hearts, was Charles, known as Charlemagne, the great Charles, King of the Franks and Holy Roman Emperor. For centuries he has been left-handed, holding his sword (which for a time was a battle axe) in his left hand, while grasping his ermine with his right. He might be considered the leader of the pack. The Jack of hearts is La Hire (1390–1443), a real knight. A friend of Joan of Arc, he was notorious as a bandit and pillager, some of his exploits being so terrible that mothers would threaten their naughty children that La Hire would get them. The current Jack of hearts in English packs is shown holding a foppish leaf or feather in his right hand, but La Hire was originally holding a truncheon. The lower part of the truncheon got lost from the card design around 1800 and the handle of it, which was slightly curved, became a leaf, no doubt by an artist's error, so La Hire now is quite out of character. He has always been moustached, and in profile, being one of the 'one-eyed Jacks', the other being the Jack of spades.

The King of spades in the 1760 Paris pack is King David, who is famous as the young slayer of the giant Goliath. He felled Goliath with stones from his sling and then cut off his head using the giant's sword. He still holds the sword, and is King of swords (*spade* in Italian). In early cards he also held a harp, which is now lost. His Queen is a Greek goddess, Pallas or Pallas Athene, the goddess of wisdom. The Jack of spades is Hogier or Ogier, sometimes called Hogier the Dane, although this is a misunderstanding, since he seems to have come from the Ardennes rather than Denmark. He was a cousin of Charlemagne, and married an English princess.

The King of diamonds who, as Alexander Pope noted in his 1712 poem, 'shows but half his face', is Julius Caesar, and he still shows half his face, having always been in profile. He was marked Caesar on playing cards as long ago as 1490. His Queen is a Biblical character, Rachel, wife of Jacob and mother of Benjamin. The Jack of diamonds is Hector, but this is a mystery. The French like to think he is Hector of Troy, but that mighty Hector would not be a mere Jack or valet. In early packs the Jack was Roland, another of Charlemagne's court. When Roland became Hector on the pack, it is most likely that he represented Hector de Maris, a noble knight who was a half-brother of Sir Lancelot, friend of the Lady of the Lake (Lancelot also belongs to the pack of playing cards as the Jack of clubs).

The King of clubs is Alexander the Great. He is the only king who has an orb, which has remained unchanged for centuries, and above which is the French *fleur-de-lis*. In early playing cards this orb was held in his right hand, which some time in the 18th century disappeared, so that on current cards the orb is unsupported and merely decorative. The Queen of clubs is labelled Argine, which is but an anagram of *regina*, the Latin for queen. She is the only genuine queen in the pack, therefore. The Jack of clubs, as mentioned, is Lancelot, the son of a French king and the chief knight of King Arthur's Round Table. Having been accidentally wounded in his rear by an arrow shot by a huntress, which he removed himself, he is depicted on early cards holding an arrow. Sadly, on modern designs, the flights have disappeared from the arrow and he holds what looks more like a pointed staff.

These, then, are the heroes and heroines who battle for us over the card table.

# Playing Cards with Children

This article deals with the practicalities of teaching children to play cards and the various types of games included in this book.

## Skills

There are many different skills needed to play cards well, and children will acquire them gradually as they grow older. Some of the skills which come to bear in playing games are:

| | |
|---|---|
| *Memory* | In many games it is an advantage to remember which cards have been played, or which cards have been taken by other players. |
| *Deduction* | In trick-taking games like Omnibus Hearts, for example, it is necessary to try to work out by their play the cards which opponents hold. An aspect of this comes into play even with simple children's games like Go Fish. |
| *Arithmetic skills* | These might be simple, as in a number of adding-up games in this book, where players have to add together the pips on two or more playing cards, or they might be more advanced, such as calculating chances in games like Pontoon. |
| *Reaction skills* | In games like Snap and Slapjack, the winner is likely to be the player whose reactions are the quickest when certain cards are laid. |
| *Psychology* | In some games being able to sense how an opponent might play is valuable. Gops is such a game. |

## Teaching children

When teaching a child to play a game it is necessary to decide what skills are required and whether the child has them. It is not necessary that a child should be able to play a game well immediately, but he will enjoy the learning more if he feels he understands what the game is about. Conversely, if he is out of his depth he could be put off cards altogether and slink back into his bedroom to his computer.

The best way to teach a child a new game is to begin to play it, where applicable, with all the hands exposed, so that if he plays a bad card it can be pointed out to him, with an explanation why another card would have been better. Let him change the card he played for a better one. Once it is thought he can hold his own, it is still a good idea for a while if an adult, who is not taking part in the game, could oversee his play and help him. It will not be long before everyone can play on (more or less) equal terms.

## Types of game

The games can be divided roughly into groups as follows:

| | |
|---|---|
| *Adding-up games* | These are good ones to start a young child on. They have the added advantage that they might polish a child's numeracy skills. Twenty-Nine is possibly the easiest. All it requires is that a child be able to count up to 29. Others only slightly more complex are Fifty-One, Obstacle Race and Jubilee. |
| *Going-out games* | Some of these games can be played by very young children. Cheat, Old Maid, Sequence and Snip-Snap-Snorem are among the simplest. Fan Tan, Rockaway, Rolling Stone and Switch are a touch more complex. As soon as |

children can play the simpler games, parents will not want to be involved. However, Cheat is a game which will produce arguments and tantrums. A sensitive but firm adult supervision therefore will sometimes prevent tears.

*Capturing games*
The opposite of going-out games, the object of these games is to capture all the cards. These are simple children's games they can play by themselves, and include Beggar My Neighbour, Snap, War, Menagerie and Slapjack. The first three in particular are among the earliest games children learn. Adult supervision might well be necessary in Snap, Menagerie and Slapjack, which can be quite rowdy and argumentative games.

*Collecting games*
These are games where players collect sets of cards of equal rank or suit, and include Go Fish, My Ship Sails, Pig and Spade the Gardener. Very young children can play these, but Go Fish in particular can bring out the worst in children who do not like their carefully collected sets of three cards of the same rank to be taken from them by a player with the fourth card of that rank.

*Matching games*
Casino, Chinese Ten and Stealing Bundles are games involving matching cards with others. Casino is a game where skill plays a part and is a good one for adults and children to play together.

*Gambling games*
Gambling games like Bango, Crazy Eights and Ranter Go Round are enjoyed by young children when playing with counters. Other games, like Farmer, Newmarket, Pontoon and Thirty-One require a little judgement and can be played with older children either with counters or modest stakes.

*Patience games*
Four Patience games are included: Accordion, Clock, Demon and Klondike. All are easily mastered by children, although all are difficult to get out.

*Trick-taking games*
Trick-taking games by nature require some degree of skill, and therefore are best suited to children of ten years or older. This book does not include Bridge or Whist, which are complex and technical, but describes a dozen other good games which parents and older children can play together. For teaching children the principles of trick-taking games, Knockout Whist is suggested as a starter. Other trick-taking games are Bismarck, Cucumber, Gops, Knaves, Linger Longer, Nomination Whist, Omnibus Hearts, Pip-Pip!, Romanian Whist, Scotch Whist and Sixty-Six.

*Other games*
Other games included in this book which are hard to fit into the above categories are Cribbage, an excellent and skilful game for two, three or four people; Pelmanism, a simple game depending on memory; varieties of Rummy, a ubiquitous melding game; and President, an increasingly popular family game for all ages, adapted from a widely played Chinese game.

A final word to parents who teach children to play games. Keep helping them until you are sure they have grasped the object of the game and any niceties of skill that may be relevant. They will think that they know it all long before they actually do. Be patient. Allow them to win sometimes if it encourages them, but do not bend the rules to help them. Do not allow them to bend the rules (or cheat!) either, even by accident. Point out that rules are rules and that games aren't worth playing if not played properly.

# Index

# Games by Number of Players

# Games by Alternative Names

# Games by Age of Players

*To Mary and Jack, my mom and dad, for making me
proud when they listened to my youthful rantings and
stopped smoking before it was too late.
It's good to still have you here.*

*To Margo, Matthew, Tanis, and Jordyn, for making
every day a joy to live and for never starting to smoke.
Your love of life is exhilarating.*

*To those with COPD whom I've been privileged to know.
Your courage is uplifting and the lessons you teach invaluable.*
— R.V. H.

*To the memories of Janet Jones, Edgar Boileau, and Audrey Maloney.*

# Contents

# *Foreword*

*C*hronic Obstructive Pulmonary Disease (COPD) is a major cause of
death and disability in Canada, affecting more than 750,000 Canadians,
and there are strong indications that as many as 1.5 million may be
afflicted. It is one of the few causes of death whose incidence has not
decreased over the decades — in fact, a four-fold increase has been seen
since 1971. The profile of COPD has changed as well — we used to think
of COPD as a disease of older men, but more and more we are seeing it
in younger people and especially in younger women — in fact, in the next
few years, women with this disease will outnumber men.

Statistics, however, do not tell the true story of COPD. COPD can be
best characterized as a disease of loss: loss of contact with people and the
outside world, loss of control and confidence, loss of identity and self-
worth, and loss of hope.

Yet it also inspires a search for renewed and newfound meaning. And
that is what *Every Breath I Take* is all about: helping people with the illness maintain or re-create satisfying, joyful, and substantive lives. This
book heralds a new era in the optimal management of COPD, and

should certainly be required reading for anyone interested in providing the best in care *and* prevention.

Many exciting developments in COPD management promise to take shape in the first part of this decade that will help sufferers, their families, and their health care providers. The Lung Association has been significantly involved in the care of people with lung disease for years. Now, by focusing on COPD, we are evolving into the first place to which those diagnosed with the disease can turn. We remain committed to facilitating the union of knowledge and expertise in COPD.

Our first step was founding the Canadian COPD Alliance, a national organization created in 1998 that provides leadership to all those with a stake in COPD. We have launched BreathWorks and our national toll-free Helpline — 1-866-717-COPD (2673) — the first project of its kind in North America to provide telephone and web-based COPD disease management led by COPD educators. We are also actively involved in the development and dissemination of new physician guidelines for the management of COPD, expected to be completed by the Canadian Thoracic Society later this year.

*Every Breath I Take* points to the many community resources available to Canadians through our BreathWorks COPD program, and we hope that every reader takes an active role in using what's available to them.

The Lung Association commends the efforts of Rick Hodder and Susan Lightstone in providing a rich and balanced approach to a largely unknown subject. *Every Breath I Take* will inspire and teach everyone affected by COPD — physicians, allied health professionals, patients, family members, and associations like ours — so that together we can forge a new future for COPD patients, one that is bright and positive. Because when you can't breathe, nothing else matters.

*Alan McFarlane, Canadian Lung Association*
*January 2003*

# *Acknowledgements*

*I* owe the inspiration for *Every Breath I Take* to all the people with COPD I've been privileged to know over the years. After the medical interview is over and the "doctoring" completed, there's always time for talk. Talk about life, family, trips planned, about feeling optimistic, about feeling alone and isolated, about feeling scared — anything goes. I've learned that everyone brings something different and unique to the task of coping with COPD.

My COPD friends have amazing stories to tell — their ability and courage in meeting the challenges of COPD continually astonish me. The idea of telling the story of COPD through their experiences grew naturally from listening to them recount the details of their lives. With their help and the efforts of Susan Lightstone, *Every Breath I Take* was born. To all of you who taught me about the real nature of COPD — the human side — thank you.

Especially warm thanks to Arthur, Audrey, Don, Edgar, Janet, Jean, Lorraine, Louise, Mychelle, Peg, and Raymond for their time and generosity in sharing their stories with us.

Many colleagues contributed to *Every Breath I Take*. I offer huge thanks to Luanne Calcutt, Kim Danovitch, Mary-Jo Lewis, Debbie

Swihart, and Karen Kinney for their aid in facilitating the patient interviews so essential to this project. From the beginning, Steve Simonot and Nozhat Choudry of Boehringer Ingelheim Canada Inc. encouraged our efforts and served as valued resources. Cindy Shcherban and Alan McFarlane of the Ontario Lung Association and Ross Reid of the Canadian Lung Association offered many helpful insights along the way.

Many people spent time and energy discussing issues and ideas with Susan and me. Thanks to Gay Pratt of Ottawa's Access Therapy Centre, Dr. John I. Stewart, Bob Elford, Kitty Wilkins of Statistics Canada, Brenda Hannivan, Carole Madeley of Lakeridge Health, and Miriam Sobel, managing editor of the *Canadian Journal of Respiratory Therapy*. To everyone at Ottawa's Rehabilitation Centre — thank you. We're particularly indebted to Dr. Douglas McKim, Colleen Kenney, Maria Watson, Dr. Peter Henderson, and Dr. Meridith Marks.

They say a picture is worth 1,000 words and we were privileged to work with two talented artists who have made *Every Breath I Take* speak volumes. Thank you to Robin Chernick for her stunning photographs and to Jeanne Simpson for her clear, elegant drawings.

Editors are the people who make our work look easy. The Key Porter editorial team of Clare McKeon and Sue Sumeraj enriched the book with their accurate and insightful comments. Thanks also to Don Bastian, Shaun Oakey, Bill Kretzel, and Barbara Sibbald for their careful attention to our work.

For many years — almost as long as we've been friends — Susan Lightstone and I talked about writing a book together. Thank you, Susan, for ensuring that our book is now more than simply a "good idea."

Finally, this project was demanding of time and commitment. It would have been impossible without the patience and support of Margo, my true love, and that of our children, Matthew, Tanis, and Jordyn, our hopes for the future. I know Susan's family — Lyon, Adrian, and Nicola — provided the same loving and supportive environment for her. Without knowing it, my parents, Jack and Mary, and my mother-in-law, Kay, also provided important help as windows on a generation to which most of my COPD friends belong. They too are wonderful examples of how the human spirit can adapt to and overcome challenges.

*Rick Hodder, Ottawa*

# *Introduction*

*B*reathing — we all do it. It's necessary for life. For most of us, it's easy to do, even when we exercise. It's so natural, we don't even realize we're doing it.

But for people with lung disease it's a different story. Every breath they take can be a struggle they must think about constantly, especially those afflicted with a disease called COPD. Chronic obstructive pulmonary disease — that's what COPD means — is a grab-bag term for a collection of diseases, emphysema and chronic bronchitis among them. All are characterized by chronic airflow limitation, or a difficulty in moving air into and out of the lungs easily.

Whether you're suffering from COPD or caring for someone who is, you know that COPD is all about catching a breath. And simply put, each and every breath counts. Easy breathing — something most folks take for granted — is often an enormous and debilitating struggle for those with COPD.

Given this fundamental fact of life that COPD patients and their caregivers face every day, we've decided to make *Every Breath I Take* a little different from what you might expect. Yes, you will find in the pages that

1

follow all the latest medical information about COPD — which drugs might prove useful, and how to keep yourself fit and well nourished, for example. But we also want to give expression to the experience of living day in, day out with COPD. So we asked eleven people who have COPD to share their stories with us — and with you.

The profiles of these individuals convey how each has learned to cope with the progression of their disease, chronicling the changes they've made to their lives, the choices they've faced, their successes and their failures. You'll also meet caregivers and partners. People with COPD do not live in isolation, and the disease can have a profound impact on family members who may find themselves cast in the role of caregiver.

As you read through *Every Breath I Take,* you'll discover these voices of experience integrated with the topic of each chapter, telling us about COPD through the eyes of people experiencing the disease. We hope their stories and the practical advice they provide will put a human face on COPD that is both encouraging and informative — like a portable support group in book form. Most important, we want you to know that you're not alone in facing the challenges that life with COPD presents. Like the name says, COPD is a chronic disease. Once you've got it, you can't get rid of it. When you're suffering from a chronic disease like COPD, both you and your family face an uncertain and difficult future.

Even though most healthy people have never heard of COPD, it causes significant suffering in North America and around the world. The World Health Organization has estimated that by 2020 COPD will be the third leading cause of death worldwide. It currently ranks fourth among the leading causes of death in Canada and, as of 1997, fourth among the leading causes of death in the United States. More than 100,000 Americans die each year from COPD, while nearly 16 million are afflicted with the disease. And more than 750,000 Canadians (3 percent of the adult population) suffer from COPD, at a cost of several billion dollars annually to the health care system. But the emotional and physical cost to the individual cannot be measured in dollars and cents.

COPD is a smoker's disease. It's not usually diagnosed until patients are in their fifties or sixties. The statistics bear this out: the prevalence of COPD among Canadians thirty-five to fifty-four years old is 1.9 percent, but it leaps to 6.4 percent in the sixty-five- to seventy-four-year-old age group. Despite a decrease in the number of people smoking cigarettes,

COPD prevalence and mortality rates are on the rise. COPD is having a big impact on women in Canada — probably because of increased smoking in this group — and it is projected that by 2005 more women than men will be dying from COPD.

Despite these grim statistics, there are plenty of people living with the disease and many of them are doing remarkably well. As a measure of the magnitude of the impact of COPD in Canada, in 1998 The Lung Association helped create a national forum called the Canadian COPD Alliance to "facilitate the development and implementation of national strategies for the prevention, early detection, and optimal management of COPD in Canada" (www.lung.ca/CCA/).

COPD is a complicated and perplexing affliction — indeed, the emotional toll of the disease can be as debilitating as its physical symptoms. This frustrating state of affairs is compounded by the widely held perception that COPD is a "self-inflicted" disease. Perhaps this attitude is one of the reasons why medical research into COPD has lagged behind that devoted to other pulmonary conditions such as asthma, with the result that available drug treatments have not had much positive impact on the treatment of COPD. In fact, many doctors still regard and treat COPD as if it were just "tough asthma," offering up the same drugs for both diseases. Such attitudes are changing as we learn more about the disease, thanks to new research initiatives.

Today, however, smoking cessation still remains the only hopeful means of altering the progression of COPD. We don't need to tell you how difficult it can be to kick the habit, but we'll strongly urge you to do just that in our chapter on smoking cessation.

There are many ways to manage your disease and, in turn, control and relieve your symptoms. As you progress through *Every Breath I Take*, you'll learn that this concept of "managing" the disease is unique to each individual — as the testimonies of our group of eleven illustrate. Depending on your experiences with COPD, your personal strategy can involve choosing a doctor who's right for you; getting adequate exercise; learning to breathe properly; preparing yourself to travel the world; eating nutritiously; maintaining a healthy weight; keeping tabs on your lung function; finding a rehabilitation program tailored to your needs; managing the stress associated with a chronic illness; and maintaining a close and intimate relationship with loved ones.

But the process of effectively managing your COPD starts with education. You need to know the what, how, when, and why of various techniques that can keep your COPD under control.

Each and every member of our group of eleven told us that learning about their disease was the first — and most important — step in living with COPD. We feel Raymond expressed it best. At seventy-four, he maintains an active lifestyle despite a diagnosis of COPD several years ago. A large medical encyclopedia sits prominently on a bookcase in the living room of his tidy apartment. Raymond refers to it often, refreshing his memory of the details of how various parts of his body work — or, as the case may be, don't work. "If you want to live with COPD and enjoy your life, you have to accept the disease. Once you've accepted it, you can begin to learn to adapt to it," he explains. "A big part of adapting to the disease is learning about it. And that means learning about how your body works.

"When I was first diagnosed with COPD, I went through hell. I was panicky. I didn't want to leave my apartment. I was afraid. My dad had died of COPD. Once he was diagnosed, he never left the house. I knew I didn't want to live the rest of my life like that. When I started to learn how my body worked, I learned what my lungs could and couldn't do for me. In other words, I started to learn my limits. I learned how far I could go. I learned how to breathe properly and how to listen to my body. But first, I had to sit down and think about things. When you're well, who cares? Your body works and you don't have to give it a second thought. But when it doesn't work well, you better start learning!"

So, how can you put *Every Breath I Take* to best use in learning about your disease? If you've just been diagnosed with COPD, you'll probably want to read it cover to cover. But each chapter is designed to stand alone as well. If you've been living with COPD for years and you're interested in learning only about the benefits of oxygen therapy, for example, head for chapter 11. If you're thinking about travelling to South Carolina for the winter, start with chapter 12. If it's time to get into shape, look at chapters 7 and 8. And so on. Refer to the table of contents, and use the index to find the topics that interest you.

Education, it has been said, is the movement from darkness to light. We hope *Every Breath I Take* will shed the light you need on the subject of COPD.

# 1

## Catching Your Breath — How the Lungs Work

"You can't understand it unless you've experienced it." That's Peg talking about breathlessness caused by COPD. "You think you're not going to get your next breath. You think your lungs will shut down. You're certain you'll die — right then and there. When I first started experiencing breathlessness, I'd panic. I had to get help right away. I had to find *someone* to help me." So, with each attack of breathlessness, Peg would rush to the nearest emergency department, looking for that someone to help her.

That was Peg's pattern for a couple of years — out of control and driven by panic — until her doctor suggested she start learning about her condition. An understanding of how her lungs worked, he suggested, would help her break her pattern of panic.

Peg took her tentative first steps by attending a respiratory rehabilitation program. "The key thing I learned," she says, "was that *I* am the someone who can help me. An integral part of that lesson came from learning the basic mechanics of the lungs — how they work and why they work that way. I now know that breathlessness is a symptom of COPD. By itself, it's not going to kill me. So, instead of running to the hospital,

I've stabilized my condition and learned to cope with many things on my own. I realize now that many of my fears about my health were fears of the unknown. With knowledge, I've conquered those fears. In the beginning, I only reacted to feelings. Now, I understand *why* I feel the way I do."

Understanding your COPD is your first step toward controlling and stabilizing its progress. Like Peg, you too can conquer your fears of the unknown with knowledge. You may not have the option of attending a respiratory rehabilitation program, but you can acquire that knowledge from many other sources, including this book. So, let's begin at the beginning. An understanding of COPD begins with a tour through the normal lung.

## *Breathing and Life*

The **respiratory system** — your airways and lungs — is a complicated, sophisticated, and very delicate system. Like any sophisticated machine, the respiratory system can easily be messed up — and sometimes impossible to repair. When it's working well, this machine functions effortlessly. Every day, the average healthy person takes more than 17,000 breaths, automatically and easily.

Without the oxygen you take in with every breath of air, you would die within a few minutes. Your body needs energy to live, and every cell in your body requires oxygen to extract that energy from food molecules. Since your body cannot store oxygen for more than a few seconds, you have to keep breathing. It's a simple equation: no oxygen = no energy = no life. And your respiratory system is responsible for bringing in the air, about 20 percent of which is oxygen. But that's only half the process.

When oxygen combines with food molecules to release energy, two waste products are produced: carbon dioxide and water. Ridding carbon dioxide from the body is just as important as bringing in oxygen. If it isn't removed from your body, carbon dioxide will eventually poison you. So, just as oxygen must come in, carbon dioxide must get out, and to do so it travels up the same respiratory path that brings the oxygen in.

The respiratory system is all about the exchange of these two gases. Oxygen is inhaled into the body; carbon dioxide is exhaled. The exchange of these two gases takes place at the very end of the respiratory system, through a process called **diffusion**. From the point when you first breathe in an oxygen molecule to the final point where it diffuses into a cell is a long journey. Let's take that trip through the respiratory system.

Breathe in. You take air in through either your mouth or your nose. Both your mouth and nose do a pretty good job of filtering out large particles — dust and bacteria, for example — from the air you inhale. Those particles are trapped in the hairs in your nose and the mucus-producing membranes of your nasal passages and the large airways of the lungs. Those **mucous membranes** contain mucus-producing glands and are lined with **epithelial cells** that have short hairlike structures, called **cilia**, on their surfaces.

The cilia are constantly moving, sweeping along the mucus that contains many of the foreign particles you've breathed in. That sweeping motion carries the mucus away from your lungs. (Most of it ends up in your stomach because you swallow it.) Together, the cilia and mucus create an efficient fil-

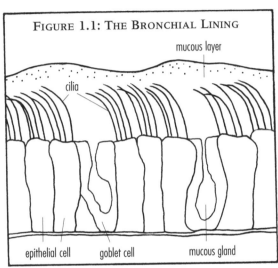

FIGURE 1.1: THE BRONCHIAL LINING

mucous layer

cilia

epithelial cell    goblet cell    mucous gland

tration system, ensuring that the delicate lungs are not contaminated by dirty air. (As you'll learn later, one of the many harmful effects of cigarette smoke is to paralyze these cilia, causing inflammation that ultimately destroys them. When this happens, the mucus can't move along the airways; the mucus builds up until you are forced to cough it out. We call this **chronic bronchitis**.)

The air moves along, entering your **pharynx**, the space at the back of your mouth, behind your nose. Food moves through your pharynx too, but is kept out of your lungs by a small trapdoor valve called the **epiglottis**. Below the pharynx, and protected by the epiglottis, is the **larynx**. The larynx is the upper portion of the main windpipe, or **trachea**. You can locate your larynx by feeling your neck for the bump that is your **Adam's apple**, a large band of gristle-like material called **cartilage** that protects the larynx from injury. (Your Adam's apple is named after the biblical Adam. While in the Garden of Eden, Adam is said to have got a piece of the forbidden fruit — the apple — stuck in his throat . . . hence the lump.) The larynx is also your voice box, containing your vocal cords. The nose, pharynx, and larynx make up the **upper respiratory tract.**

The **lower respiratory tract** starts just below the Adam's apple. The air continues to move down through the trachea, which is held open by rings of **cartilage.** Cartilage is a strong and resilient substance designed for double duty: it helps to protect the airways and keep them open. Grab your nose between your thumb and index finger, just where your nose joins your upper lip. Wiggle it from side to side. This structure separating your nostrils is also cartilage.

The trachea is about 12 cm long and about the same diameter as your thumb. At its end, it divides into two large airways called **bronchi** — the

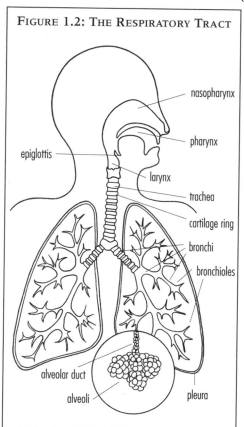

FIGURE 1.2: THE RESPIRATORY TRACT

nasopharynx
epiglottis
pharynx
larynx
trachea
cartilage ring
bronchi
bronchioles
alveolar duct
alveoli
pleura

left and right main bronchi. Like the trachea, the bronchi are made up of muscular tubes lined with mucous membrane, a soft, pink tissue like the inside of your nose. The mucous membrane contains many mucus-producing glands as well as epithelial cells lined with cilia. These glands secrete the liquid mucus that keeps the airways moist. Like the trachea, the major bronchi are partly surrounded by cartilage.

The next stop for your breath of air is the lungs themselves. Visualize two sponges, each about the size of a football. That's what the lungs look like from the outside. Each lung is covered with a thin layer of tissue